Cyburbia

Cyburbia

The Dangerous Idea
That's Changing How we Live
and Who we Are

JAMES HARKIN

Little, Brown

LITTLE, BROWN

First published in Great Britain in 2009 by Little, Brown

A CIP catalogue record for this book
is available from the British Library.

Hardback ISBN 978-1-408-70114-0
C-Format ISBN 978-1-408-70113-3

Typeset in Garamond by M Rules
Printed and bound in Great Britain by
Clays Ltd, St Ives plc

Papers used by Little, Brown are natural, renewable and
recyclable products sourced from well-managed forests and certified in
accordance with the rules of the Forest Stewardship Council.

Mixed Sources
Product group from well-managed
forests and other controlled sources
www.fsc.org Cert no. SGS-COC-004081
© 1996 Forest Stewardship Council
FSC

Little, Brown
An imprint of
Little, Brown Book Group
100 Victoria Embankment
London EC4Y 0DY

An Hachette Livre UK Company
www.hachettelivre.co.uk

www.littlebrown.co.uk

To the memory of Rose Harkin

Contents

Preface

The first time I began to wonder about our whole approach to understanding digital communications, I was having sex on Second Life. It was 11 October 2006, and I had my reasons. Second Life, for anyone unfamiliar with it, is the most visually impressive of a new generation of social-networking sites that have grown up all over the net in the last decade. Its new users are invited to create an avatar, or visual persona, and then guide that avatar through three-dimensional landscapes in which they can chat to other avatars and teleport themselves anywhere they care to go. On a single day in Second Life you can buy virtual clothes, fly a virtual plane and even enjoy virtual sexual liaisons within designated areas. I was there to report on the place for the *Financial Times*, but almost everyone else I met seemed to have an equally valid reason for being there too. Surrounded by palm trees, carefully cultivated beaches and gorgeously dressed virtual women, there were whole armies of us clueless avatars – marketers, writers, publishers, academics, technology geeks and designers – wandering around with strict instructions to sample whatever exotic delights Second Life had to offer. As droves of reporters piled into the place to find out what was going on, the colourful copy that came back made for bracing reading. It was, in retrospect, the closest I'd ever come to being a foreign correspondent.

The most interesting thing about Second Life, however, wasn't anything that went on there but the fact that we wanted to spend time there at all, ceaselessly pressing buttons in an effort to engage with strangers on an online network. One reason why our understanding of mobile phones and the internet is such a Disneyland of escapist metaphors – when we are not deemed to be cruising along an information highway we are voyaging into cyberspace, beaming ourselves into the virtual world or storming the electronic frontier – is that the experience of using a mouse to manoeuvre a cursor across a computer screen, or of jousting with the buttons on a mobile phone to reply to a text, seems so utterly dull. This is a shame, because the real story of how our new communications equipment came into being is more diverting and more revealing than any of the metaphors cooked up by technology gurus. The apparently humdrum act of moving a cursor across a computer screen, for example, can be traced to the efforts of a mathematician called Norbert Wiener to build a more responsive anti-aircraft gun with which to shoot down German bombers during the Second World War. Since the enemy pilot was continuously zigzagging around to avoid anti-aircraft fire and the anti-aircraft gunner was constantly having to adjust his aim to keep up, Wiener concluded that the best way to think about it was to understand that we humans were slowly becoming messengers on a continuous information loop, agile and highly responsive to whatever new information crossed our path. If we are to understand what our new digital gizmos have made of us, and the intensity of our involvement in them, we could do worse than imagine ourselves as that anti-aircraft gunner, constantly adjusting our aim in response to a stream of messages about the direction of the enemy pilot – or as that pilot, sitting in a cockpit amid a mass of flickering lights, manoeuvring in response to a continuous loop of information about the gunfire chasing us from the ground.

The idea of ourselves as messengers navigating an endless loop of information is called cybernetics, and this book is the unauthorised biography of that idea. It is a story that is nearly seventy years old, and telling it will take us from bombing raids during the Second World War all the way through to the war in Iraq and the 2006 Israeli invasion of South Lebanon. Passed through the hands of three influential disciples – Norbert Wiener, Stewart Brand and Marshall McLuhan – cybernetics has inspired not only the development of our new communications equipment but a distinctive approach to life, the universe and everything. From its military origins, it was given a new lease of life and an enormous fillip when its ethos was borrowed by counter-cultural agitators amid the air of global rebellion in 1968. It infiltrated the hippie communes that sprung up around San Francisco in the wake of that rebellion and, when many of those same hippies went on to become prime movers in the development of the computer industry and the internet, it duly became the poster boy for that industry as it helped to transform the economy in the eighties and nineties. As computer networks found their way everywhere and began to acquire a warm metaphysical glow, it was cybernetics and its successor discipline, network theory, which persuaded many thinkers that we humans could be treated as information processors on a giant social network. Not only that but, as we grew up hitched to computer games, mobile phones and the internet and got used to wandering around on their electronic information loop, cybernetics welded itself to our very sense of perspective. A distinctively cybernetic aesthetic has burrowed its way into the stories we watch on TV and in the cinema, and a cybernetic sensibility is also finding an echo in everything from alternative theatre to football to the organisation of the mainstream media. In the early years of this century, many fanciful ideas about human nature cooked up by cybernetic and network theorists became somewhat self-fulfilling when we strapped ourselves into online social networks and began to pass information between us as human nodes on those networks.

The story of cybernetics is important not for its own sake, but because the architecture of our digitally connected world was built on its foundations. The electronic information loop that its prophets imagined would tie us all together has, to a large extent, now been built. Starting from the beginning and working its way up, this book excavates the ideas of cybernetics in the hope that they can shed some light on what it does to us to spend time on that information loop. It is a tale about how technology is shaped by ideas, and then how our experience of that technology, together with our understanding of those ideas, goes on to shape the world we live in. In some ways our story is an heroic one. Cybernetics, after all, owes its origins to an audacious attempt to beat back enemy aeroplanes intent on bombing a civilian population. To its cheerleaders, its progress has been an epic march towards a global electronic village in which, for the first time in human history, each of us would be capable of communicating with each other directly and as equals.

It hasn't, however, quite turned out like that. En route to its futuristic electronic village, this book argues, cybernetics dropped us off in Cyburbia. Cyburbia is the place we go when we spend too much time hooked up to other people via a continuous loop of electronic information. The contours of this place can be traced directly to the architectural plans laid out long ago by the gurus of cybernetics. The time that we spend with electronic information is not making us stupid, coarse or illiterate, and what follows is not just another colourful journey into the fantasies we construct for ourselves in our virtual lives, nor an exposé of the terrible things that go on under the cover of the internet. Rather, it is about our attachment to electronic information itself, and what it is doing to us back in the real world. When Marshall McLuhan argued that the medium is the message nearly half a century ago, he meant that the content of a medium is often less important than the difference it makes in us just to have it around. It was a good point, but McLuhan didn't live long enough to see his aphorism twisted around. The world we now inhabit is one in which messages are rapidly becoming the medium: electronic messages sent back and forth between us at breakneck speed on a never-ending electronic information loop. More than just a place, Cyburbia is the state of limbo induced by living in thrall to this information loop – a state whose repercussions, as we will see, take us far beyond our fantasy second lives and well into the first.

Introduction

Imagine that a man is sitting alone at a table in a thinly furnished room. We don't need to know this man's name or what he looks like, but let's call him Mr Black. What we do know is that Mr Black has been here for quite some time, sitting limply in front of a typewriter and trying to write a report that desperately needs to be written. Things, however, are not going to plan. After several months of sitting, day after day, in front of this typewriter Mr Black has very little to show for his efforts. He is, however, a determined man. In search of some inspiration he decides to move both his desk and the typewriter on it nearer to the window.

Not that there is very much to look at. Mr Black's window opens out on to a terrace of identical three-storey houses. From where he is sitting, rows and rows of them stretch out in both directions, a grid of rooms and windows that goes on as far as the eye can see. It is not much of a view, but he is grateful for it anyway. If he is honest with himself, it makes him feel less alone. Sitting at his desk after dinner one evening, however, Mr Black happens to notice a light on in one of the rooms just opposite, and what seems to be a woman sitting at a desk by her window. At first Mr Black is only curious (is this another writer with something pressing to say?) and then he begins to think that something about the woman's face looks familiar (is she an acquaintance? Has he seen her around?) and so, little by little, Mr Black begins to take an interest in the movements of his opposite number.

Mr Black's interest in his anonymous prey across the street is all the more curious because she does not seem to do very much. She walks around the room a little and makes herself cups of something, but for the most part she just sits at her table staring at a typewriter not dissimilar to his own. With few distractions, however, Mr Black is happy to take this phantom writer – think of her as Miss White – for a metronome, a regular movement whose rhythm he can write to in the absence of anything else. He is at a loss to decipher any rhyme or reason in Miss White's actions, but there is something tantalising about having such a close connection to someone who doesn't know that they are being watched. Slowly, but with the galvanising force of a chemical addiction, Mr Black becomes obsessed by Miss White. At great length and in great detail he begins to wonder who his opposite number is and what she does when she is not working at her desk. Lonely and a little bored, watching Miss White helps keep him awake and alert because now he has something to look out for. After all, who knows what might happen next?

Except that nothing happens next. Day after day Miss White simply stares at her typewriter, paces up and down the room and then sits back down at her typewriter to assume the writing position. It is at this point that Mr Black begins to notice that Miss White seems to be staring in his direction. Mr Black can't be sure – she is across the road, after all, and concealed behind a pane of glass – but it seems to him that Miss White might be becoming as interested in him as he is in her. For one thing, she starts wearing more suggestive clothing – short skirts, tight-fitting T-shirts, that kind of thing – and walking around the room with more grace and more deliberation. One afternoon, which Mr Black has not forgotten readily, she spent the whole afternoon writing in what seemed to be no more than a bra and knickers. For his part, Mr Black begins to take more care in his appearance: he shaves more regularly and gets into the habit of checking how he looks in the bathroom mirror before he sits at his desk. It's difficult to tell, but before long it seems to him that Miss White might be smiling in his direction, and so he starts smiling back. Not only that, but she begins turning the lamp on her desk on and off repeatedly, sometimes in rapid succession, and Mr Black convinces himself that she is trying to tell him something.

But what can she be trying to tell him, exactly? Mr Black begins flickering his lamp on and off in immediate response to her flickers. For a time Miss White seems to reciprocate, alternately switching her lamp on and off as soon as Mr Black has done so, but all of a sudden she stops. Blaming himself for failing to make his message understood, Mr Black begins to switch his lamp on and off again to attract the attention of Miss White, but to no avail. Miss White is still there, but she seems to have lost all interest in what Mr Black is trying to say. Then Mr Black resorts to subterfuge. He is a little ashamed of himself for doing it – it is so very unlike him, he thinks – but for the best part of a week he turns his light off all day and all evening and hunkers down out of sight so he can appear invisible to Miss White and continue to stare at her without being noticed. It makes little difference. Miss White is still flouncing around in her flat as if she is still being watched, but there is no longer any reason for her to believe that she has Mr Black as a spectator. It is only then that Mr Black notices a flicker coming from a room several houses down the street, and then another flicker coming from a different floor in the same house, and then what seems like the shadow of a flicker coming from several houses along on his own side of the street. At this juncture it dawns on Mr Black that either he is not the only party to this exchange, or – and this prospect strikes him as even more sinister – his eccentric flirtation with Miss White is not the only one taking place between those who live on this street.

After a long time standing at the window weighing up these alternative explanations, Mr Black decides that the answer probably lies somewhere between the two. He is out-raged, but his anger burns out quickly. The fact is, he has begun to enjoy being a witness to the daily routine of Miss White, even if he is not the only one enjoying the view. More importantly, Mr Black has now noticed another person to be interested in, a Mrs Pink who keeps scowling in his direction and seems to be cross with him. Maybe she is a friend of Miss White, Mr Black thinks in a moment of paranoia. Then there is Mr Grey, who is also writing at a desk, one floor down from Miss White, and who begins holding up handwritten notes for Mr Black to see. He is, Mr Black thinks, trying to tell him something about Miss White.

Mr Black is still fascinated by Miss White, but now there are Mrs Pink and Mr Grey to think about too. And there will be others; friends of Mr Grey, for example, whom Mr Grey will be happy to point him in the direction of. Mr Black's little adventure with Miss White seems to have acquired its own momentum because before very long what he took for a mundane suburban street is now a mass of flickering lights and people sitting at windows. Mr Black doesn't like to think about it, but the project he set himself and which once seemed so important has now been completely forgotten. Now he has something else to think about, something at least as demanding as his work. But just how else is he to keep in touch with all these new friends?

Let's forget about Mr Black and Miss White for the time being. They are important not for what they do but because of the relationship between them and how they try to communicate with each other. Alone in their respective rooms with only a window to look out on the world, they make for an exact architectural replica of a place most of us have already been but can't quite put our finger on. Owing to the peculiar way in which they have got to know one other, Mr Black and Miss White's relationship is exactly analogous to that of the relationship between two nodes on a computer network. What happens to them is exactly what happens to human beings when their relationships are translated into the form of electronic information and funnelled along copper wires and wireless channels. To a great extent, Mr Black and Miss White are what we have all become.

But outside of the strange catalogue of circumstances that led Mr Black and Miss White into such a merry dalliance, why should a human relationship ever turn out like this? Despite what some people would have you believe, humans do not naturally behave as if we lived our lives on a computer network. For the last thirty years some thinkers and technology enthusiasts have been working to extend an awkward metaphor borrowed from computers into human relationships. Much of what they said was tendentious and unhelpful; a good portion of it was plain wrong. Over the course of the last decade, however, as both the technology and our behaviour caught up, their theories finally made something of a quantum leap from clumsy metaphor to reality. They did so because, no longer content with staring at garish websites on a computer and sending the odd e-mail to our friends, millions of us took to spending great tracts of our time hooked up to a vast online information loop – mainly on sites like eBay, Google, Facebook, Second Life and YouTube – populated and governed by ordinary people like ourselves. In doing so we volunteered ourselves to act as human nodes ferrying information back and forth on a vast electronic information loop – and, at least for the time we spent there, we would find ourselves behaving as such.

I call this place Cyburbia. Cyburbia is the place we go to when we hitch ourselves to electronic information for long periods of time, and online social networks are only its most visible manifestation. But why Cyburbia? One of the most important developments of the late nineteenth and early twentieth centuries saw the slow but steady exodus of the population from cities to suburbs, that peculiar no man's land located outside of town but within its general orbit. Helping all this along were amazing new transportation technologies– the train, and then the car – which enabled people to connect up their lives and their jobs in the city with their new homes in suburbia. Suburbia began life in the minds of planners, engineers and architects, but the momentum of its growth took its cue from the spontaneous decisions of city-dwellers to up sticks and relocate there in search of a better quality of life. They escaped to suburbia because they wanted to spread their wings, to enjoy untrammelled space and a greater sense of community outside the confines of the city limits. Despite many of the criticisms levelled against it, suburbia is where most of us now live.

This book is not about suburbia or how it has developed in the last hundred years. Places are what we make of them, but they are also determined to some extent by ideas we have about them, and the distinctive planning and architectural decisions that flow from those ideas. Just as the train and the car gave rise to the suburbs in the twentieth century, what follows will argue that a new kind of technology – the communications gadgetry of mobile phones and the internet – has precipitated a mass electronic migration to Cyburbia at the beginning of the twenty-first. Just like suburbia, however, it took a spontaneous flight of real people to make those plans a reality. For much of its early life, suburbia was characterised as a place full of secrets and intrigue, punctuated by fitful attempts among strangers to get to know one another. Not much used to happen there; at least not a great deal appeared to be going on. Beneath the surface and under cover, however, it was a different story – one of scandalous gossip, illicit encounters and the endless twitching of curtains. So it is in Cyburbia.

This is all very well, but however can it help us understand the peculiar case of Mr Black and Miss White? Sitting in their respective rooms with only a window for company, they become distracted by each other and begin a kind of communication. In the terminology favoured by technology enthusiasts, Mr Black and Miss White are not only peering at each other: they are also peers for each other. What that means is that both get to ferry messages back and forth via their respective windows without any need for an intermediary or chaperone. What develops between them is known as 'peer-to-peer' communication – between equals on an entirely level playing field.

There is something else that strikes the casual observer about this communication between Mr Black and Miss White. With no chaperone to chivvy their relationship along and pass messages between them, the momentum of their relationship grows entirely spontaneously and at their own initiative. Each stokes the curiosity and intrigue of the other, which ensures that both of them continue to come back to the window for more. There is one final sense in which Mr Black and Miss White are peers for each other, too. Since they have not been put in touch with each other by any matchmaker, each enjoys a degree of anonymity. At any point, either of them could get up out of their chair, slam the door shut behind them and forget about anything that may or may not have gone on between them. With their real identities carefully concealed, both Mr Black and Miss White are free to make up their identity and appearance as they go along. As anonymous peers, both know instinctively that their appearance from their respective windows is the most important thing they should attend to. It is, after all, the first and perhaps only thing that their peers will see.

Why does all this matter? In the same way that Mr Black and Miss White serve each other as peers on a primitive network, Cyburbia is a place in which communication has been ironed out into something perfectly flat and non-hierarchical. Since information is now passed back and forth between peers there, every kind of authority is levelled or demolished. Just like the relationship between Mr Black and Miss White, the kind of equality forged among peers in Cyburbia is usually rooted in their anonymity. Many people go there, in fact, because they find this anonymity liberating, or because they want to spend time in a place that allows them to define themselves rather than be defined by others. There is something else distinctive about the peer-to-peer architecture that has sprouted in Cyburbia: since there is no central messenger or administrator and everyone who is plugged into Cyburbia at any given moment is responsible for passing information through the system, this is a network that runs not only on electricity and computing power but on human activity. One consequence of that, as we shall see, is that its residents need to remain frenetically active participants in order to keep their homes in the place alive.

Why does Mr Black become obsessed with Miss White, a woman he doesn't know and whom he is not even sure knows that he exists? The short answer is that, having opened up a dialogue based on the implicit exchange of messages, he has got it into his head that he needs to keep that dialogue alive. In the strange relationship that develops between Mr Black and Miss White, messages between them can only circulate within the space between the two windows by which they sit. One way of putting it is to say that the space between those two windows has become the information loop, something closed off from the rest of the outside world and the only way in which signals or messages between the pair can circulate. Having entered into that information loop, Mr Black becomes obsessed with closing it and awaiting the next message.

The messages that Mr Black is so keen to send back into that information loop are called feedback. When we think about feedback today we are reminded of all those forms we are asked to fill in when we sample products or services. The idea, however, started out with a more specific meaning, which comes from the engineering of electrical systems. Feedback is simply information that is fed back into any system in instantaneous response to information that comes out of it, and an information feedback loop is the arrangement which makes that possible. The idea of feedback helps explain the almost gravitational pull that grips people and pulls them back, again and again, into Cyburbia – and why they begin to feel twitchy when they haven't logged in. In the same way in which Mr Black is drawn to the window to reciprocate previous signals or messages sent to Miss White and requite her apparent interest in him, the compulsive urge to return to Cyburbia arises as a result of a pressing desire, having sent a signal there, to return to close the circle of our previous engagement with the system and return feedback. It is important that we do, because information feedback loops are the glue that holds much of life in Cyburbia together. People who buy or sell items on the internet auction site eBay, for example, are encouraged to complete a form giving feedback on everyone with whom they do business. The idea is to sow feedback loops – to introduce an element of reciprocity into the system and thereby help stabilise its operation.

Sometimes it works; just as often it fails. The idea of feedback will help explain why communication in Cyburbia so often breaks down into rancour and confusion. If a continuous cycle of messaging and feedback is so important in maintaining a system of communication, then the breakdown of that cycle – as Mr Black discovers – can often make us tetchier and more abrupt in the messages that we send. At worst, it can lead to a self-perpetuating spiral of misunderstanding, anger and abuse.

Think one last time about the relationship that develops between Mr Black and Miss White. The two might well be very interesting to those who know them, but thus far they know next to nothing about one another. Neither is there anything in the way their relationship has evolved to suggest that they will get to know each other any time soon. All this is immaterial because, as nodes on a network, their personal characteristics are left behind. What matters to the network is only that they have forged a tie or connection with each another, and that they can use that tie to zip messages back and forth between them.

The tie established between Mr Black and Miss White is certainly weak, and it does not seem to have done them many favours so far. Worse than that, the puzzling mode of communication that has grown up between them has actively hampered their attempts to communicate with one another. That, however, is only one way of looking at things. The tie between Mr Black and Miss White is weak, but through his encounter with Miss White, Mr Black has also become acquainted with Mrs Pink and Mr Grey, both of whom will prove to be valuable sources of gossip not only about Miss White but about other people on the street as well. Add up all those myriad ties between Mr Black, Miss White, Mrs Pink and Mr Grey and we arrive at an explosive array of connections, which the network can use to push information around the place at lightning speed. It is not the individual ties or connections, in other words, that are fortified by all this frenetic activity between the residents of our street. They stay as weak as they were, while the network grows ever stronger. Mr Black has slowly become more immersed in the game of flickering lights with Miss White and the others than the report that he initially set himself to write. But if Mr Black were telling the truth, it is not that he is in thrall to Miss White, Mr Grey and all the others as individuals. It is the communication and the chatter itself that has become his passion, even as it has escalated from a titillating distraction into an all-consuming game of strategy.

The fate that has befallen Mr Black is not so different from what happens to all of us when we spend too much time in thrall to an information loop in Cyburbia. Plugged into Cyburbia, we combine face-to-face interactions and friendships with loose ties to an electronic diaspora throughout the world. These are people who we don't usually know, but whose trace in the electronic ether is only a degree of separation away from our own. In Cyburbia these are our weak electronic connections, and they diffuse information around the globe more much rapidly than stronger, face-to-face relationships would have done in the past. But what kind of information do they diffuse? The same kind of malicious rumour that would have been smothered by stronger relationships flows more easily through a network of weak ones. The links between us in Cyburbia are certainly weak but, as we will see later, they are made no stronger by the plethora of different connections forged there. Quite the opposite. What becomes more powerful is not us but Cyburbia itself; it draws its strength from the weakness of those myriad ties and then, emboldened by all the information rushing through it, goes on to use it in sometimes amazing and sometimes perverse ways. This is all very well for the continued growth and development of Cyburbia, but meanwhile the ties that bind us to each other and to it begin to chafe. The danger is that, bound together in a network of loose electronic connections and drawn slavishly to Cyburbia for our inspiration, we end up in something not unlike an electronic chain gang.

Let's leave Mr Black and Miss White where they are, staring mutely at each other from just across the street. To understand why anyone ever thought the development of this place called Cyburbia might be a good idea we need to excavate and dust off the ideas from which it was built.

1

The Loop

What does it mean to be in the loop? In the summer of 2004 researchers from the technology company Yahoo! gave twenty-eight Americans notebooks and asked them to spend two weeks without access to the internet or other communications gizmos, and to record their thoughts and movements in a diary. When those diaries were handed in the results made for intriguing reading. So much had the study participants begun to rely on the internet that many had forgotten that resources such as the phone book, newspapers and telephone-based customer service were even available. Many of them complained about the inconvenience of having to look up numbers in the phone book, or of dealing with paper documents such as airline tickets. Without Google to see them through dull afternoons in the office, many were at a loss as to know what to do with their time. Three out of four said they spent more time talking on the phone, watching TV or movies and reading newspapers. Some reported visiting their neighbours more, others that they spent more time exercising. So eager was one man to get his old online life back that he told researchers 'I'm even looking forward to seeing spam.'

Much more keenly felt than the loss of the internet as a means of looking up information, however, was the feeling among the subjects of the study that they had been shut out of a communications loop. 'I haven't talked to people I usually talk to and have been tempted to go on instant messenger because I feel out of the loop,' complained one study participant, Kristin S. 'I'm starting to miss e-mailing my friends – I feel out of the loop,' said Penny C. One chatroom discussion on the study quickly descended into something like Alcoholics Anonymous, as heavy users of the web queued up to confess their hopeless dependence on electronic communication. 'Hi, my name is Spak,' announced one, 'and I'm an internet addict . . . I usually only experience withdrawal when I'm in a place where I can usually get internet access but for some reason can't at the moment (i.e., the power goes out at home or the network goes down at work). I have literally started shaking because I couldn't check my e-mail at work. Sad.' Another chatroom user, calling himself John McKenna, was quick to chip in. 'After reading this article I found how true it was to my own life. I can't remember the last time I ever said "Hi" to one of my physical neighbours, let alone a conversation. Some people can spend their whole night tapping away on the keyboard. I myself have done this on several occasions. I do not watch television any more. I sit right down in the computer chair and start typing in web addresses. I like the fact that I can go anywhere while surfing the web, unlike television where there are set programs.'

John McKenna and Spak were right about their dependence on communications gizmos; it's just that they were a little misinformed about the underlying causes. Whatever guilt-ridden users of the internet might think, it makes little sense to think of them as addicted in the way that people become chemically dependent on heroin or nicotine. A better comparison is with the time that people spend watching television. Many of us still watch a lot of TV, but few would argue that it is addictive in any meaningful sense. What it does for the most part, however, is to supply its audience with visual stories of different kinds, and we continue to watch it because we want to piece those stories together into something with a beginning, a middle and an end.

The time that we spend chattering with other humans on the web or via our mobile phones, however, is something else entirely. In this new medium we may still be searching out stories (we will get to that later) but what we get are other people. Why, then, do we continue to go back for more? Somehow we must have developed a pressing need for regular electronic communication with other people. Just as Kristen and Penny said, more than anything we need to stay in the loop. For at least thirty years the idea of being in the loop has meant no more than being in the know, privy to information known only to those in a hallowed inner circle; to be cut out of the loop, by contrast, is to be distanced from your colleagues and excluded from a circle of power. The general notion of being in the loop, however, is even older than that. To properly understand what it means we need to reach far beyond mobiles and the internet, much further back in the twentieth century and into the middle of a world war.

*

In 1940, shortly after its fighter planes had been repelled by the Royal Air Force, the Luftwaffe unleashed an onslaught of punishing bombing raids on London, the ferocity of which stunned the entire world. The first raids came in the afternoon of 7 September and were concentrated in London's densely populated East End. About three hundred bombers attacked the city for over an hour and a half, and hundreds of fires lit up the sky. The night bombing that followed lasted for eight hours, shaking the city to its foundations with the deafening noise of hundreds upon hundreds of exploding bombs. Faced with this new and seemingly unstoppable kind of slaughter delivered from the air, the citizens of London began a mass exodus into the countryside.

To British army scientists, the situation looked grave. The problem was that military aircraft had become so fast and so flexible since the First World War — the most advanced German bombers flew over their targets at speeds above three thousand miles per hour, and at altitudes as high as thirty thousand feet — that anti-aircraft gunners on the ground had their work cut out to catch them. Worse, the pilots of these mighty new aerial bombers had become expert in taking evasive action, constantly veering off onto a new trajectory to outwit the efforts of the gunners below. There were about ten men in the average British anti-aircraft artillery unit. A spotter was charged with spying the plane through binoculars and keeping it in view, and then relaying its position to the unit's mathematicians who would calculate the plane's projected location and pass those coordinates to the gunners; in turn, the gunners would rotate their heavy turrets into position using hand cranks and fire a volley of shells in the general direction of where the plane was thought to be headed. The task was one of prediction: of estimating the future position of a fast-moving aircraft based on its past and changing position, of calculating the range and targeting factors and finally of firing the anti-aircraft gun with enough precision to blow the bomber out of the sky. The process was listless and cumbersome in the extreme, and usually succeeded only in missing its target and wasting a valuable shell.

Thousands of miles away from London, news of the success of the bombing raids and their civilian casualties pricked the conscience of a mathematician called Norbert Wiener. Wiener was the son of an eccentric Jewish schoolteacher who had emigrated from Poland to America and had settled in Kansas to start his own alternative vegetarian community. A prodigy and a polymath, Wiener had been awarded his doctorate at Harvard at the age of eighteen and by the thirties had settled down to mathematical work at the prestigious Massachusetts Institute of Technology (MIT) and even began tinkering with plans to build a primitive 'electrical network system' – an early computer. All the while he longed to play a more active role in the unfolding calamity that he was certain was about to engulf Europe. So profoundly did the persecution of European Jewry affect Wiener that he sought help from a psychoanalyst to resolve his emotions. Nor was he shy of subterfuge: even before the outbreak of war he was privately floating the idea that he and other scientists should send letters detailing fictional conspiracies to zealous pro-Nazi scientists so as to confuse the Nazis and perhaps even put some of their best scientists behind bars. With the actual outbreak of war, however, everything changed. Soon after hostilities began a group of British technical experts and military officials went to America with their secret plans for a high-resolution radar device that improved upon America's existing technology for finding planes in the air. The Brits offered their know-how to the Americans in return for advice on something more pressing – how to improve their unwieldy anti-aircraft systems. The problem, as the Brits well knew, was not only one of calculating where the planes would be in the sky, but of building an electrical contraption to bring those ever-changing predictions back to the anti-aircraft gunner as soon as they were arrived at.

Norbert Wiener, who had begged his superiors for some years to put his considerable brain at the service of the war effort against the Nazis, had found his project. Motivated by the chance to add something real to the battle against European Fascism, Wiener shelved his attempts at building a primitive computer and applied himself immediately to the task. Together with Julian Bigelow, a promising young engineer at MIT, he set to work on the anti-aircraft fire problem using only a blackboard on which to scribble his calculations. Japan's sneak attack on Pearl Harbor in December 1941, which brought America into the war, only added urgency to the project. By the summer of 1942 the pair had produced a prototype flight path predictor machine, which was far more accurate than anything that had gone before. Even with accurate information, however, the problem was how to get the gunner to adjust his aim accordingly – to connect that predictor back to the battery of anti-aircraft guns and to modify the operation of all this heavy machinery in response to a continuous loop of information about both the zigzagging flight path of the plane and the system's performance.

In search of a device that could automatically translate predictions about the flight paths of bombers into action on the part of the anti-aircraft gunner, Wiener and Bigelow travelled from Boston to airbases in Virginia and North Carolina. They spent hours patiently watching aircraft in flight and the movements of gunners who manned anti-aircraft units on the ground. Observing the workings of not only the steering mechanism of anti-aircraft guns but of the gunners themselves, the philosopher in Wiener began to become a little obsessed by the implications of what he was up to. This idea of feeding a continuous stream of information about the flight path of the plane as well as the anti-aircraft gun's performance back into the targeting apparatus, it struck him, could best be thought about in terms borrowed from engineering and electrical circuitry. The streams of information that were being fed back to the gunner to improve his performance, after all, looked very much like feedback loops in an engineering system. For Wiener, the immediate advantage of seeing the movement of the anti-aircraft gunner and the firing system in mechanical or engineering terms was that he could go on to model the operation of the firing mechanism using mathematical formulae. However, as a mathematician and philosopher rather than an engineer the idea was, for him, freighted with much broader implications about the relationship between man and electrical machine. The gunner, his firing system and the anti-aircraft flight path predictor machine, Wiener began to believe, could all be seen as embedded in the same system of continuous feedback, one in which information about the system's output – its firing performance – along with information about the flight path of the plane was continually being processed and fed back into the system to improve its aim. But that wasn't all. Just like the gunner, the enemy pilot depended on a continuous loop of information about both his own direction and the direction taken by the anti-aircraft fire. Looked at from the outside, it was as if gunner, pilot and their respective machines had all been fused via an information loop into a new kind of self-regulating system akin to a thermostat, a thing of almost natural beauty that constantly righted its errors through feedback from its environment. This new information loop between man and machine was becoming so fluid and harmonious that Wiener began to imagine it as entirely self-steering and automatic.

The prototype electrical anti-aircraft predictor machine that Wiener eventually produced made use of feedback loops to improve the system's performance. Just as Wiener suggested, the contraption worked by thinking of the anti-aircraft gunner and the enemy pilot as adversaries bound together in a single information loop or system, and then used electrical circuits to feed back to the gunner a continuous loop of information about the attempts of the pilot to move out of the gunner's line of fire. When the prototype was demonstrated for military commanders, it impressed them greatly. As Wiener candidly admitted, however, the improvements which would be necessary to convert his prototype into a working model would require more time and resources than could in all conscience be diverted from the war effort, and so the system was held in abeyance while the war progressed. It would take another decade for the American military to build and deploy their first anti-aircraft missile system based on Wiener's cybernetic principles but it eventually proved a success. Seventy years later the principles of cybernetics are still a valuable inspiration to military weapons manufacturers everywhere.

By the time his machine was fully built, Norbert Wiener had moved on. He was still a committed anti-Fascist, but he had grown suspicious of the power of the American military-industrial establishment to influence the control and direction of scientific work. As early as 1944, Wiener had made so many enemies within the National Defense Research Committee (NDRC) that he was in effect sacked from military projects. Wiener's gloom intensified as he witnessed the fruits of his cybernetic research being used for more and more destructive military purposes, and he convinced himself that human society was spiralling out of control and heading towards inevitable apocalypse. He never worked for the military again, and gradually became a staunch critic of the militarisation of modern societies and the emerging Cold War. The use of atomic bombs in Hiroshima and Nagasaki in 1945 so disturbed him that he even wrote a letter tendering his resignation from MIT.

Wiener never got around to sending that letter. Instead, he seems to have decided that the only way to slow society's hurtle towards self-destruction was by harnessing the idea of the continuous information loop of instruction and feedback which was, he felt, the only worthwhile legacy from his years of research on behalf of the military. Furthering his analogy between self-steering engineering devices and human action, Wiener began to see feedback loops everywhere. The picking up of a pencil, for example, was a process in which information from the eyes was processed by the nervous system to control the hand. The driver of a car, likewise, could be seen to be steering his car away from possible collisions, continually looking out for obstacles and passing a continuous stream of information back into the physical motion of turning the steering wheel, all the time monitoring the consequences of his actions and feeding that information back too. As early as

1942, and after discussions with a physiologist friend, Arturo Rosenblueth, Wiener had adapted the Greek word *kybernetes*, which means 'helmsman' or 'pilot', to explain all this. The new science of cybernetics would deal only in messages and their transmission; it would, Wiener announced, be 'the study of messages as a means of controlling machinery and society'. It would no longer be limited to engineering systems and could equally be applied to messages sent by people, electric motors, pieces of machinery or the brand new electrical computing machines that scientists were then in a race to build.

Wiener could not claim to be the only one to have noticed the new importance of both messages and the systems for sending them. Even before war had broken out, scientists on both sides of the Atlantic had increasingly come under the control of government, whose officials offered huge amounts of money for projects that might conceivably be of military use. As social scientists and linguists were mobilised and encouraged to rub along with scientists and engineers, the result was a ferment of interdisciplinary activity. The technology to which academics now had access suggested to many among them that there might be hitherto unacknowledged similarities between machines and organisms, particularly between high technology, growing computerisation and the human central nervous system. John von Neumann, for example, the American mathematician and polymath who went on to invent game theory, had been working hard to build the world's first general purpose computer; like Wiener, his experiences had convinced him that parallels might be drawn between the brain and a computer, and the prospect that logical theories might emerge from computerisation which could help to explain the workings of both. So proud was Wiener of his theory of cybernetics that he wrote to von Neumann to suggest that they jointly convene a small group of scientists to talk about questions of common interest. Von Neumann enthusiastically agreed, and the first meeting of the Cybernetics Group took place in March 1946 at a hotel in New York. Twenty-one of America's top scientists, including Wiener and von Neumann, sat around a table and talked for two days about the changing relationship between man and technology that seemed to have emerged from the fruits of their wartime research.

A total of ten conferences were held by the Cybernetics Group between 1946 and 1953. They took place amid a flush of patriotism and paranoia, at a time when the United States and the Soviet Union were gearing up for a new war of military stealth, and are now seen to have played a crucial role in the development of the human and natural sciences in the post-war period. Not least, they helped to bring Norbert Wiener's pet discipline to new audiences and inspired him to take his theory to giddy new heights. At one of the conferences, for example, Wiener expressed the hope that cybernetics might help with the development of prostheses for those who had lost a sense or a limb. And as if to underline the implication that cybernetics could be used for peaceful as well as violent ends, Wiener even tried to use his theory to translate the sound of speech into a tactile sensation for the deaf via a special glove that would be worn by the deaf person. The glove was not a great success, but Wiener's prototype for the design proved influential and he is now considered a pioneer in the field of prosthetics.

Not surprisingly, however, Wiener's most memorable attempt to synthesise what he had learnt during his wartime experiences lay in theory rather than in practice. In 1948, two years after the first meeting of the Cybernetics Group, Wiener published *Cybernetics, Or Control and Communication in the Animal and the Machine*. The book was a dense thicket of equations and all but incomprehensible to the layman. In the book and his more accessible follow-up, *The Human Use of Human Beings: Cybernetics and Society*, Wiener tried to tease out the idea, implicit in his theory of cybernetics, that communication and messages were central to an understanding of what it is to be human. What sociologists had hitherto overlooked, Wiener posited, was the extent to which society is based around the communication of information. Advances in the transportation of information such as the telephone and the radio in the early twentieth century had shown beyond doubt that man was, above all, a talking animal. Political philosophers of the nineteenth century had seen humans as essentially productive creatures, but Wiener's experience had convinced him of the centrality of messages. Ever since the invention of the steam engine, he noted, artists and thinkers had been entranced by the relationship between machines and the human muscle that they seemed to be replacing. The development of new kinds of sophisticated electrical machines, which had gathered speed since the outbreak of war, Wiener continued, was giving rise to a new kind of industrial revolution – and if these new machines were going to mimic the capacities of real humans it wasn't going to be human muscle but human information processing. Didn't the emergence of these machines and primitive computers show that machines, just like humans and animals, had the capacity for language and the sending of messages? It was now quite possible for a machine to talk to a machine, just as it was possible for a human to talk to a machine, and, despite his underlying humanism, Wiener drew the conclusion that messages between humans, animals and machines were now of the same fundamental nature. Just like machines, human actions of any kind could be modelled as a never-ending information feedback loop in which the actor, like a puppet on a series of strings, would continually adjust himself to messages fed back to him about both his environment and his effect on that environment. In *The Human Use of Human Beings*, Wiener illustrated the import of messages by drawing upon his relationship with his cat:

> I call to the kitten and it looks up. I have sent it a
> message which it has received by its sensory organs, and
> it registers in action. The kitten is hungry and lets out a
> pitiful wail. This time it is the sender of a message. The
> kitten bats at a swinging spool. The spool swings to the
> left, and the kitten catches it with its left paw. This
> time messages of a very complicated nature are both
> sent and received within the kitten's own nervous
> system through certain nerve end-bodies in its joints,
> muscles, and tendons.

Like Pavlov's dog, Wiener's cat would have no easy life. So excited was he with the possibilities inherent in the electronic message that he even mulled the possibility of sending a live human being through some kind of electronic communications system. Given that the individuality of a body is written in our genes, he argued in *The Human Use of Human Beings*, 'there is no absolute distinction between the types of transmission which we can use for sending a telegram from country to country and the types of transmission which at least are theoretically possible for transmitting a living organism such as a human being'. Sending live humans over the telephone network, however, proved too onerous a task even for Wiener. 'That we can't telegraph the pattern of a man from one place to another,' he concluded wearily, 'seems to be due to technical difficulties, and in particular to the difficulty of keeping an organism in being during such a radical reconstruction.' The idea itself he thought 'highly plausible'.

With its whiff of science fiction and Wiener's portentous prose style, the idea of cybernetics was soon all the rage among intellectuals, writers and artists. Despite its fearsome complexity, *Cybernetics* soon became a bestseller; readers began to identify with it and to see cybernetic feedback loops all over the place. Even though he expressed it in the desiccated language of a mathematician, Wiener saw cybernetics as a sincere attempt to improve the human condition and save it from possible entropy, or planetary chaos. It is impossible to understand Wiener's writing in the forties without a nod to his intellectual pessimism, which is never far from the surface: his work is shot through with tragedy and foreboding. 'In a very real sense,' he tells us, 'we are shipwrecked passengers on a doomed planet.' However, the problem was not technology but what we humans made of it. All that was needed, Wiener felt, was a clear understanding of what human purposes are and how we could accomplish them. The new science of cybernetics was crucial in this because it was ideally suited to revealing how inadequate communication might lead a society to fly off the handle just as it might cause a car to career out of control. Like the car driver, the only hope for human society was that it might act to correct its mistakes and steer itself, through endless feedback loops and constant monitoring, away from danger. After all, he believed, didn't the answer to most problems or mistakes, whether in humans or machines, lie in better and more regular communication?

Norbert Wiener died in 1964. Towards the end of his life, disappointed by the climate of fear engendered by the Cold War, he retreated further into his own writing and his rather apocalyptic theories about encroaching chaos and disorder. By now a round, bespectacled man snappily dressed in tweeds and well coiffed with a goatee beard, Wiener looked like a cross between a Surrealist painter and Inspector Clouseau. Tales of his bumbling absent-mindedness became legendary on the MIT campus. 'Do you remember the direction I was walking when we met?' he is reported to have asked one student. 'Was I going or coming for lunch?'

Long before the invention of the first personal computers in the seventies, Wiener has good claim to be the first-ever computer geek. His notes on the anti-aircraft problem became one of the founding texts in a new science of information and communication theory. The complex equations he worked on to advance his theory of cybernetics also helped to crystallise a revolution in communications engineering as routine operations of all kinds became increasingly automated through feedback loops.

Not least among Wiener's legacies was his idea of the loop. The image of being 'in the loop' is usually traced to America in the seventies, but probe a little further and you can trace everything back to Norbert Wiener. It was, after all, Wiener who was the first to suggest that the language of information loops favoured by engineers and electricians could be made to apply to humans as much as it could to machines. Along with the loop, it was Wiener who gave us the now ubiquitous notion of feedback. Central to his new science of cybernetics, remember, was the principle that the whole of human society could be imagined as a system regulated by the looping flows of information around it and the continuous feedback that they brought. Nowadays we are constantly being asked by companies, institutions and authorities to give us feedback on their workings. Buy something, take evening classes or have any dealings with a government department and you are very likely to be asked to feed back information on your experience so it can improve what it does. When we do so, we are implicitly paying homage to Norbert Wiener's cybernetics and the idea that we inhabit machine-like systems that require continuous feedback for their smooth operation. This kind of feedback is easy to ignore but, as the technology with which to give feedback matures and our attachment to the idea grows, the information that we send back to those in authority is being taken more seriously than ever. But, as we shall see later, feedback does not always make the system run more efficiently. Moreover, those institutions that do most to invite it often get more than they bargained for.

Wiener's new discipline of cybernetics would turn out to be uncanny in its ability to predict how computerisation would affect human society, and deeply influential among those who would go on to build those computers and hook them up via the internet. Such is his influence that one way of seeing the entire web of communications technology that we rely upon today is that it arrived from the barrel of a gun – in this case, a fully automated anti-aircraft gun that brought man and machine together in a whole new kind of collaborative harmony in an effort to take a stand against Nazism. In principle, Norbert Wiener was entirely in favour of electronic systems usurping all manner of human tasks – automated machines, he well knew, could only make life less onerous. Just as he predicted, increasing automation and computerisation have made information loops and feedback more and more important in monitoring all kinds of processes and systems. In the end, however, Wiener could not control the genie that he had let loose on the world when he invented his science of automation through feedback loops. There was little he could do, for example, to prevent the military from using cybernetics to improve its sophisticated missile guidance systems.

Militarisation was not the only danger that Wiener felt confronted a society which controlled itself automatically through a system of feedback loops. Even in the forties, Wiener was warning of the possibility that an over-reliance on automation and computerised technology might blight the human condition as well as ameliorate it. His chief concern was that automation would lead people to surrender to the machine their own purposes and their powers of mind. The danger would arise 'when human atoms are knit into an organisation in which they are used, not in their full right as responsible human beings, but as cogs and levers and rods . . . in machines'. In light of how our relationship with electronic information would develop, Wiener's worry that we would end up as slaves to an electrical machine now looks much more plausible than it did when he first voiced it. But why would anyone want to see themselves as a fully automated cog in a system, dependent, like a pulley, on a constant and circular loop of information for their operation? The answer, as we shall see in the next chapter, lies in the kind of information that courses through the system, and the kind of people who want to share it.

2

The Peer

In October 1999, at the height of a dizzying, unprecedented gold rush in internet stocks, a formerly shy eighteen-year-old called Shawn Fanning found himself at a rave in the San Francisco Bay Area and having the time of his life. Fanning had been living in the area for only a month. At the rave, however, surrounded by pulsating techno beats and the cream of the Bay Area's beautiful youth, he already felt he had discovered his spiritual home. It helped that he was high on Ecstasy; that he was beaming at everyone who moved; and that his new company, Napster, was sponsoring the event.

Fanning had moved to San Francisco from his native Massachusetts at the insistence of one of his investors. It was, after all, where any ambitious high-tech start-up needed to be. Just a few months before the move, he had dropped out of his studies at Northeastern University in Boston where, in common with his fellow technology geeks, he had been spending most of his waking hours hooked up to internet chatrooms with his music blaring in the background. Cannily, Fanning realised that he could bring his interests together by assembling a central index of the music that his friends had on their computers, so that they could all share their favourite songs via the internet. After weeks spent hammering code into his computer, he emerged with a program that, through a series of twists and turns, would go on to change the face of technology.

In the chorus of enthusiasm for all things internet-related to which everyone sang along in the last years of the millennium, Napster stood out as one of the cleverest. It was also – it didn't take a genius to work out – thoroughly illegal. In the two years before it was sued out of existence for theft of copyright, Napster found global fame and seventy million very grateful users, most of them around the same age as Shawn Fanning. Even more influential, however, was what happened after it was forced to shut its doors. To maintain a central list of his friends' music collections, Fanning had bought an internet server and a website, and it was this that did the work of letting people access each other's music. Napster's role was akin to that of an old-fashioned telephone switchboard operator, taking a request for a song from one person and connecting it up with someone else who would be happy to oblige.

But what if there was no telephone operator and no central server to shut down? Aware that any site from which they downloaded music was liable to be heavily fined and then put out of business, some of the millions who had fallen in love with Napster had a brainwave. What they discovered was that, if people didn't work from a centrally managed list of music and instead hooked up their internet connections to one other directly, it would be much harder for the authorities to catch them and make an example of the manager. Quietly

and apparently spontaneously, a new generation of so-called
file sharing systems sprang up to let people swap music without any need for a central server. These new systems became
known as peer to peer operations, meaning that they put ordinary users – or peers – together without the need for a central
chaperone. In turn, these peer-based file-sharing systems –
with names like Kazaa, LimeWire and BitTorrent – would
also come under pressure from the authorities for infringe-
ment of copyright. Since they acted not as managers of a
central list but only as electronic matchmakers, however, they
would be much harder fish to catch.

The millions of young people who, since 2001, have spent
hours hooked up to peer-based music sharing systems might
have expected a telling off from their parents for their shame-
less flouting of the law. Many of those middle-aged baby
boomer parents, however, were no strangers to schemes for
outwitting the authorities themselves. A good number of
them remembered their salad days in the sixties with fondness, and had begun to identify themselves – sometimes long
after the event – as serial up-enders of authority and continued thorns in the side of the establishment. One way of
seeing what teenagers like Shawn Fanning were up to, in
fact, was as an unconscious echo of what, thirty years previously, had been an equally stubborn act of rebellion by their
parents.

'Bogside, Clydeside,' went one popular British anarchist slogan
of the late sixties, 'join the Angry Side.' In the years since,
1968 has become synonymous with radical politics, riots, barricades and a flowering of youthful self-expression that shook
the world's political establishments to their core. The reason

this outburst of youthful anger so puzzled governments and establishments was that they had no idea where it came from, what these protesting young people wanted and what they really stood for. The Cold War, it seemed to the protesting students, had give rise to its own kind of hierarchical organisation: faceless, anonymous, top-down bureaucracies run by shady cabals of middle-aged men. Spurred on by the successes of the civil rights movement, and the prospect of nuclear annihilation, the ongoing horrors of the war in Vietnam and the stiflingly rigid nature of office life, this new breed of radical began to rage against what they saw as a cold, soulless and technocratic system that kept everyone spinning as cogs within it. Hostile to both the military industrialised bureaucracies in the West and the fossilised Communist governments of the Soviet Bloc, what became known as the New Left had little patience for either. 'They condemn Soviet society just like bourgeois society,' complained an editorial from the French magazine *Paris Match* on 27 April 1968. 'Industrial organisation, social discipline, the aspiration for material wealth, bathrooms, and, in the extreme case, work. In other words, they reject Western society.'

Having made enemies of the entrenched bureaucracies of East and West, the rebellious students of the New Left talked a great deal about democracy and the need for grass-roots participation. For the most part, however, they were not joiners. Much more than the socialists and communists who came before them, these energetic new arrivals nursed an instinctive suspicion of state power and public institutions, and, kicking against the suffocating weight of history and inevitability that coloured the official Communist view of history, they wanted to show that they could make a difference in the world, by changing people's minds. Not only were they suspicious of both sides in the Cold War, but they nursed a withering disdain for traditional forms of hierarchy, authority and political organisation. Their slogans were all about spontaneity, consciousness-raising, relentless activism and self-organisation. The means, too, were very different. The New Left preferred to disseminate its message not with propaganda-laden pamphlets but through the publication of underground papers, even via ensemble theatre groups that did their best to provoke involvement on the part of the audience. For many of them, breathing democratic life into society's austere and moribund institutions was a waste of time; the only solution would be to abandon them in favour of something else.

The political iconoclasts of the New Left were not the only radical players to come alive in the ferment of 1968. Based in New York and San Francisco, and with significant groups of supporters in Britain and in mainland Europe, an alternative, freewheeling counter-cultural movement rose almost inexplicably to the surface at around the same time. Whereas the political animals of the New Left wanted to raise awareness of social ills, these hippies wanted only to expand their own consciousness to something more humane and more meaningful. Their tools would be anti-establishment music, eastern religion, psychedelic mysticism and a smorgasbord of 'mind-expanding' drugs taken with copious quantities of free love. Whereas the intense young revolutionaries of the political movement wanted to organise themselves and everyone else – albeit in alternative institutional forms – the mavericks and hipsters of the counter-culture wanted to do their own thing and see if anyone joined in. Even more so than the young pretenders of the New Left, the hotchpotch of bedfellows who made up the counter-culture were suspicious of leadership of any kind. During an exchange of letters with a radical firebrand in 1968, John Lennon put it very well: 'You smash [the system] and I'll build around it.'

The passion and imagination of 1968, however, was gone almost as soon as it had arrived. The momentum of this 'revolution in the head' over-vaulted itself and the ensuing frustration gave way to disorientation and political violence. By 1969, for example, the American branch of the movement, Students for a Democratic Society (SDS), had split in two, and had given rise to Weatherman, an urban guerrilla group that launched a campaign of bomb attacks against business interests. As barricades gave way to bombs and the political New Left exploded into fragments, the hippies, mystics, performers and pranksters of the counter-culture were also coming to terms with a newly hostile cultural atmosphere. In 1969, when the San Francisco hippie and guru Charles Manson and his cultish followers were found to have been behind a campaign of brutal murders, the whole idea of a counter-culture held together by hippie ideals seemed to lose all its innocence. If the mavericks and hippies had ever wanted to share their wisdom and their alternative culture with mainstream society, now more than ever they wanted to retreat, regroup and take a closer look at themselves. The way forward, they began to believe, was to escape from the attention of the authorities by living in small, close-knit egalitarian communities – usually rural or semi-rural – where every member would be bound together by a shared mindset and shared ethics. Many of those who had revelled in San Francisco's Haight-Ashbury neighbourhood and its infamous

Summer of Love in 1967 had soon left for a new, communal life outside the confines of the city. Between 1965 and 1972, somewhere between several thousand and several tens of thousands of communes popped into existence – 'The largest wave of communalization in American history,' says the San Francisco academic Fred Turner.

When they left their lives in the city behind, the hippie and alternative movements wanted to wash their hands not only of racism, the arms race and the war on Vietnam, but the whole hierarchical edifice of Western society and its spurious ideas about authority and objectivity. Hadn't the chief propagandist of the new-age movement, Theodore Roszak, in his 1969 book, *The Making of a Counter Culture*, demolished the 'myth of objective consciousness' and the notion that there was an objective set of circumstances and standards around which citizens could rally their arguments for change? If a new and alternative Jerusalem had to be built, these veterans of the counter-culture were going to build it outside the reach of mainstream society, and from the ground up. What they were seeking in communal living was a greater egalitarian sensibility and an escape from toweringly bureaucratic mechanisms for social control, which seemed to them to be dwarfing all that was good about American society. What they hoped to create was an alternative new world in which citizens could learn to relate to one other in more authentic and more humane ways. Little by little, and without anyone really noticing, a movement to raise people's awareness of social ills had turned in on itself, and morphed into one whose aim was to forge a more direct kind of communication between like minds.

*

In 1968, while political radicals were marching against the war in Vietnam and the commandos of the counter-culture were still enthusiastically tearing down the boundaries of good taste, a twenty-nine-year-old bohemian and drifter called Stewart Brand was busy printing off copies of a magazine and driving them around San Francisco in a pick-up truck. Having graduated from Stanford University eight years previously, apart from a two-year stint in the US Army and a spell at the San Francisco Art Institute, he had been wandering ever since. Brand was the offspring of middle-class, eminently respectable folk. His father was an advertising copywriter and his mother an amateur radio operator, and the combination seems to have instilled in him an understanding of the power of communication. Like the student activists he saw around him, Brand had struggled for a way out of the suffocating dualism of Soviet state socialism and Western bureaucratic capitalism, and had begun to seek alternative avenues for free expression and the development of individual freedom. Brand's particular intellectual coming-of-age had taken the form of a decade-long traipse through a wide variety of radical, creative and bohemian communities in New York and San Francisco. In the early sixties, that journey had taken him to an itinerant collective of artists called USCO ('The Company of Us'), where he worked fitfully as a photographer and a technician to create 'happenings', or apparently spontaneous celebrations of technology and mystical community. It was the enigmatic Brand's first encounter with life in a hippie collective. USCO was a fusion of eastern religion, ecology and thinking about systems, and, drawing on everything from strobe lighting to electronic displays, it sought to create art that might change the consciousness of its audience: in a promotional flyer for a 1968 performance in New York, USCO advertises itself as 'uniting the cults of mysticism and technology as a basis for introspection and communication'.

But how did troublemakers from the counter-culture, many of whom had been railing against technology for turning citizens into automatons, allow themselves to believe that it might be a force for good too? The truth was that the attitude of sixties radicals to technology and the media had always been ambivalent. One of the slogans daubed by the protesters on the walls of central Paris during the riots of 1968 was the injunction to be 'neither a robot nor a slave'. On the other hand, many protesters were deeply conscious that technology and the media might eventually be used to fight against 'the system' as well as to perpetuate it. Many hippies could see the point of it too: one way of looking at lab-manufactured LSD, after all, was as a highly portable new technology capable of transporting its users to a better place. These technology-friendly hippies drew much of their inspiration from the cybernetics of Norbert Wiener. In the twenty years that had elapsed since Wiener had invented his cybernetic information loop, it had been appropriated not only by the military but by radicals and artists. One such enthusiast for both technology and the work of Wiener was Gerd Stern, the founder of USCO. Like Wiener, Stern was a European Jew and an émigré, and in Wiener's work on information loops he had found a valuable source of inspiration for what he was trying to do with his art. It was through his work at USCO, too, that Stewart Brand arrived back at Norbert Wiener and the theory of cybernetics that he had first encountered at Stanford. Brand had studied evolutionary biology, a discipline that in the decades after the Second World War had been heavily influenced both by the new discipline of information theory and by cybernetics. Something about his work at USCO, and his involvement with Stern, must have re-ignited in Brand a sense of its possibilities. It was easy to see the appeal. After all, Brand and his fellow performers and pranksters in the counter-culture were profoundly anti-elitist and were seeking an alternative to hierarchical bureaucracies. In its own way, Wiener's vision of society had no room for hierarchies either: his perfect society was a looping circle of information and feedback that would, like a living system, seamlessly correct its own errors and ensure a better flow of communication among all those involved in it.

Wiener's vision seemed to offer nothing less than a prototype for the kind of society that the radicals would like to build. If changing consciousness and the contents of people's minds was the aim, then the free flow of information would surely be a vital ingredient, and in that case new technology could hardly fail to make itself useful. Not only that, thought some counter-culture aficionados, but the continuous information loop promised by Wiener would be better achieved outside of the purview of the authorities in small, intimately knit communities. It was not only the Americans who were discovering the radical potential of cybernetics. While Stewart Brand was busy making friends among San Francisco's radical bohemians in 1968, the most talked-about exhibition in London was called 'Cybernetic Serendipity'. Held at the avant-garde and iconoclastic Institute of Contemporary Arts, the exhibition sought to understand how cybernetics could reinvent poetry, dance, sculpture and animation, and featured a range of amateur cybernetic devices capable of responding to feedback from the audience. The exhibition attracted forty thousand visitors; so popular was it that the organisers were forced to extend its run to two months.

Europe, however, was only ever a ramshackle outpost in the struggle to bring Wiener's cybernetic vision into practice; the real action was always in California. As more and more refugees from San Francisco's demoralised counter-culture retreated from the cities to hunker down in communes, many of them brought with them not only ideas about fomenting a shared, radical consciousness outside the manipulation and control of elites, but also an understanding of the power of information, especially if it could be used to put power back into the hands of the people. Just as the academics in military think-tanks had already done, many of them began to borrow the rhetoric of cybernetics: imagining societies as systems, and the gathering and distribution of information as key not only to the world of computing and engineering devices but also to the idea of what it is to be human. Like modern fron-tiersmen, many of these battle-hardened veterans of the counter-culture had left behind both city and society to build a new kind of community of the mind, one that would be based on the seamless and continuous transfer of information between peers. They were going to find a new system for communication, which would be egalitarian and looping rather than top-down and which would burrow around the interference of the authorities with an information loop of its own. Armed with the fruits of Wiener's research, they would have no qualms about deploying local and small-scale tech-nologies to help them out.

USCO wasn't the only inspiration for the young Stewart Brand. At one point, commissioned to take photos for a brochure, he ended up at an Indian reservation in Oregon and left deeply impressed by the Native American way of life and community. He also knew and spent time with the legendary writer Ken Kesey (whose novel *One Flew Over the Cuckoo's Nest* had been published in 1962), and his Merry Pranksters, whose experiments in psychedelic mysticism and enthusiasm for LSD were subsequently made famous in Tom Wolfe's book *The Electric Kool-Aid Acid Test*. By 1968, however, Brand had had his fill of dipping his toes in the counter-culture and wanted to do something that might make a difference. He had long had the knack of cultivating interesting people from a wide variety of different backgrounds and bringing them together. As many of his friends from San Francisco's counter-culture moved out into rural areas to begin their experiments in communal living, Brand had the idea, armed with a small inheritance, of starting a catalogue or a brochure as a resource to help bring them together. In the spring of 1968, while so many of his friends were busy trying to bring down Western civilisation, Brand was searching local bookstores, writing to publishers and identifying items for his first catalogue. Together with his wife Lois, a Native American mathematician, he also took the time to drive out to visit the communes that were mushrooming in the hills around San Francisco.

The *Whole Earth Catalog*, which emerged from Brand's experiment in publishing, was something entirely new to mainstream American life. A hotchpotch of articles and features about everything from new electric gizmos to outdoor gear that might come in handy for those sheltering from the elements, it resembled a cluttered jumble sale of items, each of which seemed to bear no relation to the next. What the *Whole*

Earth Catalog liked best was information about tools, especially tools that, like the *Catalog* itself, could be made readily
available at low cost. Many of the items on offer in its pages
were simply other magazines or books, which offered readers
the chance to share perspectives or ideas. Buyers were encouraged to send in their own suggestions for features, or to
respond to other people's reviews of devices, or simply to
describe experiences that might conceivably be of interest to
other readers. As an example of the kind of small-scale, DIY
technology it wanted to champion, the *Whole Earth Catalog*
was a principle as well as a product – it was, after all, a living
demonstration of a system designed to permit the free flow of
information and feedback, whose architecture could be traced
directly back to Norbert Wiener. Much of what made it fresh
was Brand's stubborn refusal to provide his readers with a
linear and conventional path through the information within
its covers. None of the eclectic items stuffed into it bore any
relation to those on either side of it, and the whole thing
seemed to be held together by some topsy-turvy law of logic
known only to those hippies and cybernetics geeks who had
produced it. It was, according to one confused reviewer, 'held
together by some mysterious principle of internal dynamics,
some inscrutable law of metaphysics which I simply didn't
understand'. That mysterious principle was nothing other than
cybernetics. One of Brand's friends and long-time collabora-
tors, John Brockman, recalled visiting Brand in Menlo Park,
California, while he was preparing the first edition of the
Catalog. While Brand's wife Lois busied herself working on the
Catalog, he and Brand, according to Brockman's account, sat
together religiously reading and underlining a copy of Norbert
Wiener's *Cybernetics*.

The principles upon which the *Catalog* was founded may have owed a debt to the cybernetics of Wiener but that was hardly their only influence. They were also perfectly in keeping with the egalitarian ethos of the counter-culture. So involved had its contributors become in making suggestions for future articles and writing for it, that the *Catalog* soon seemed to be publishing itself. Making good use of Brand's many friends in different places, the appeal of the *Whole Earth Catalog* spread far beyond the hippie and psychedelic communes of the San Francisco Bay Area to embrace the vibrant art scenes of New York and San Francisco, and technology departments within the universities and in industry. The *Whole Earth Catalog* rapidly became a self-sustaining enterprise aimed at encouraging the direct and spontaneous swapping of information among wildly different groups of people who could meet as peers in its pages, with Brand and his pick-up truck as the all-important link in bringing them together. In so doing, it floated a new way in which its readers could relate to one another that didn't have to involve living in the same place – being part of a community of peers or equals, feeding information into and receiving information from other like minds via a continuous information loop. As a tool for the easy distribution of information among a geographically diverse audience, it would be no exaggeration to say that the *Whole Earth Catalog* was an early prototype of what online social networks would go on to become.

The *Catalog* was a publishing sensation. Within three years of its birth it was selling a million copies and Brand himself was being profiled in *Time* magazine. Its reputation had spread, and it was being bought all around the country by mail order and in bookstores. Quietly, however, all talk of politics and

even society seemed to have slipped from the picture. In the
late sixties there were nearly half a million American soldiers
in Vietnam, and American riot police were not shy of battling
radical students on campus. If everyone else was worried about
America's fractured identity, there was little if any discussion
of it in the *Whole Earth Catalog*. Not only that, but, in cele-
brating the power of technology to remake things anew, issues
of race, gender and class were strangely absent. In 1970, one
critic was moved to write in to complain about the lack of
politics. To his credit, Brand readily published the letter,
and in his reply he pointed out that the *Catalog* was not
about telling people what to do, but about giving them the
tools to talk among themselves and hopefully to organise a
way forward. If this was a kind of politics, it looked to
Brand's critics like the absence of any politics at all. It was,
however, very much in keeping with the spirit of the enterprise. What the *Whole Earth Catalog* was about, Brand had
decided, was bringing people into direct communication
with each other as equals. To do anything more would be too
prescriptive, and would look like manipulation from on high.
In keeping with the counter-culture's turn inwards, the
Catalog's rhetoric of expanding people's consciousness through
the sharing of information with their peers had become an
end in itself, and one that could do without the messy and endlessly disputable world outside.

The *Whole Earth Catalog*, in keeping with the restless,
mercurial imagination of its progenitor, went out on a high.
On 21 June 1971 Brand invited five hundred staff, contributors and friends to San Francisco's Palace of Arts and Sciences
for a 'demise party' and a 'surprise educational event'. When
his guests arrived they were confronted with a procession of

entertainers: clowns, trampolinists, even a band churning out a combination of Irish jigs and Tibetan temple music. For most of the evening the tall, wiry Brand moved through the crowd without shoes or socks, wearing a black cassock. Then he approached the stage and announced, through an intermediary, that he had twenty thousand dollars in hard cash – the profits, presumably, from the *Catalog* – to give to anyone who could think of an idea for how to use it to further the good work begun in its pages. Over the next couple of hours more than fifty people queued up to offer their views as Brand stood on the stage, still dressed in his monk's robes, diligently writing down each suggestion on a blackboard. As time wore on and the audience thinned out, no one seemed to be capable of adding up all the suggestions into a decision on how to spend the money. By the following morning, moreover, five thousand dollars of the money was found to have gone missing, and those few who had reconvened were still no closer to any agreement on what to do with it.

Brand's 'educational event' was audacious and big-hearted, but it also highlighted some of the weaknesses inherent in the *Whole Earth Catalog*'s cybernetic organisation. With everyone busy swapping information and ideas, it was often difficult to know how to arrive at an overall decision and move forward. There was another problem with how the *Catalog* had developed, too, one that went to the heart of its cybernetic ethos. Stewart Brand had drawn his inspiration from the idea that the free flow of information and feedback around a system was vital for its survival, and had borrowed it to build a self-sustaining publishing operation driven by a healthy cycle of information and feedback among the swelling ranks of its readers. As the *Catalog* went from strength to strength, it became clear that Brand and his trusty pick-up truck were never going to be enough to deliver it to all its subscribers, and Brand was forced to fall back on mail order and bookshops for its distribution. The whole point of his radical experiment in self-publishing had been to evade the clutches of the traditional authorities and put Whole Earthers in direct contact with one other. As the *Catalog*'s readership increased, its cybernetic principles became the first victim of its success.

With Brand as its champion, Norbert Wiener's cybernetics had won a fresh lease of life and a new anti-authoritarian impetus. The idea, however, was still badly in need of a technology reliable enough to act as a medium and tie its many new enthusiasts together. It would shortly find one. At the end of all that haggling over how to spend Brand's money, the few remaining Whole Earthers voted to give what remained of the money to an activist called Frederick L. Moore, who promised to keep it safe until everyone could reconvene to decide what to do with it. No one seems to know what became of the money. What is known is that the man who volunteered to safeguard it soon moved on to what many Whole Earthers had already decided was the natural way forward – setting up a computer company.

3

The Tie

In the middle of the nineties, a small group of conscientious young researchers at MIT took to lugging around whole computers and radio transmitters in their rucksacks. They wore electronic gadgets close to their bodies, digital displays in the frames of their glasses, even carried little keyboards in the pockets of their clothes. Their aim was to be permanently connected to information via the internet and electronic gadgets at all times, to be 'always on'. Anyone who queried what this was all for was told that they were in the process of morphing into cyborgs. Whenever anyone plucked up the courage to ask what they meant by that, they replied that a cyborg was the perfect cybernetic organism, a new kind of human consisting of a biological core surrounded by a penumbra of wire and electrical extensions that tethered it to the rest of the world. The word cyborg dates from 1960, when it was used by a pair of research scientists to refer to the perfectly self-regulating combination of human and electrical machine that they thought we would all have to become in order to adjust to travel in outer space. When they adapted the concept for life on planet earth, the MIT researchers found that all the extra weight they were carrying around caused them discomfort, bruises and lacerations. They carried on regardless. They were, after all, learning whole new ways of being, slowly shedding their human skins to become a wholly new hybrid of man and electrical machine. Given such an important and promising line of work, who would want to complain about a few scratches?

Fifty years after Norbert Wiener invented cybernetics in a laboratory in MIT, his disciples were busy sculpting that theory into perfect human form. The notion of a community hitched together via a constant cycle of information and feedback had come a long way since the *Whole Earth Catalog*, and its enthusiasts had hit upon the perfect way to develop it. What they discovered was a vibrant new electronic medium, made up of computers, mobile phones and the internet, through which we humans could attach ourselves to an unexpurgated flow of information from anyone who wanted to be in touch. In the mid-nineties this electronic tie was only in its infancy, which was why it was being given a test-run by some of the brightest sparks in academe at MIT. The MIT researchers claimed that, when it was ready, it was going to give rise to a whole new way of living, one in which we were more vividly and pressingly attached to our media and each other than ever before. This idea that electronic media was set to intensify our relationship with each other and the rest of the world was not entirely new. It was, in fact, the invention of yet another cybernetic prophet, an eccentric Canadian professor of English literature called Marshall McLuhan.

*

In 1968, while the radical students were doing their utmost to tear down Western civilisation and Stewart Brand was beginning his low-tech experiment in practical cybernetics, Marshall McLuhan had departed his base in Toronto for a one-year professorship in New York. He was much in demand. Bored with his native discipline of modernist literature, McLuhan had become fascinated by modern life, and particularly the creeping influence of the broadcast media. By the late sixties, McLuhan's artful generalisations and sweeping prognostications about how electronic media were about to change the fundament of society were attracting an avid and highly fashionable audience around the world, no more so than among the radical American students, artists and thinkers who were hungry for ideas about how to foment social rebellion. Buoyed up by his new status as a celebrity academic, he was flying around the world to spread the word about the coming media revolution. By 1968, McLuhan had met with Timothy Leary, the notorious evangelist for the joys of LSD, and had even gone on a speaking tour with techno-artists at USCO, who were so influenced by his writing that they volunteered to build an anarchic multimedia backdrop for his lectures.

On the face of it, Marshall McLuhan was an odd choice for the high priests of the counter-culture to champion. Tall, angular and with a fondness for dressing in tweed, he looked like a slightly effete gentleman rogue. To the students who crowded his lectures and hung on his every pronouncement, he must have seemed like some antiquated Oxford don who had, almost by accident, managed to beam himself into the far distant future. As a highly conservative Catholic, McLuhan was scathing about the prevailing mood of student activism. When one progressive Canadian cleric began to talk up the church's solidarity with the oppressed, McLuhan accused him of having 'unemployed emotions' that were too eager to be press-ganged into an entirely misguided crusade. He held conservative views on abortion, bemoaned the Vatican's recent modernisation of the Catholic mass, and had little quarrel with the ongoing American war in Vietnam. In 1968 the radical activist Abbie Hoffman declared that 'the Left is too much into Marx, not enough into McLuhan', but McLuhan did nothing to repay the compliment. Similarly, his encounter with Timothy Leary seems to have made no impression on him at all. Leary, on the other hand, remembered the encounter very well. His famous counter-cultural injunction to 'turn on, tune in, drop out', Leary claimed, came to him in the shower the day after his meeting with McLuhan, and was inspired by McLuhan's tip that LSD was never going to take off unless he thought up a tagline with 'something snappy' to promote it. Years later Leary was given to quip, perhaps having had time to read some of McLuhan's more obtuse ruminations on the media, that LSD would be wasted on the noble professor since, if the tenor of his works were anything to go by, he was already as high as a kite.

What Marshall McLuhan did have in common with the counter-culture was his debt to Norbert Wiener. He had stumbled upon Wiener's book, *Cybernetics*, as early as 1950 and, throughout the following decade, while Wiener hosted the conferences of the Cybernetics Group in New York, McLuhan and a small research team at the University of Toronto tried to develop the theory of cybernetics to understand the evolution of modern literature. Such was McLuhan's enthusiasm for the subject that before long he had left behind the study of literature entirely in favour of a study of the information containers in which that literature was housed. By the time he published *The Gutenberg Galaxy* in 1962, he was arguing that the media had always been the pivot on which society turned, and that the invention of Johann Gutenberg's printing press over five centuries earlier had given rise to almost everything that we now take to be fundamental to modern society. The mechanisation of writing that accompanied the invention of the printing press and moveable type, McLuhan argued, had brought with it more than a few job losses among the monks who served as manuscript writers. It had precipitated the demise of the oral tradition of storytelling and helped to develop languages; it had fostered individualism by making millions of books available to large numbers of people to read on their own; it had even imposed a level of standardisation in the use of language. The clearly sequenced and ordered way in which books were produced and then read had gone on to reconfigure almost everything. The growth of a bureaucracy, the linear sequence of industrial processes that characterise the modern factory and industrial life, even the nation-state – all these, according to McLuhan, had been thrown forward like a roll of dominos by the book.

McLuhan's technique was to combine paradox and rhetorical exaggeration, a lively interest in popular culture with the occasional blast from the literary canon. His genius was to write about the media in a whole new way, ignoring its content and turning instead to the machinery of the medium itself, pointing out how it had shaped us in ways that we had hitherto failed to appreciate. It was hardly a coincidence that he was one of the first of a new generation of academics who were as much at home in the television studio as they were in the lecture room. His definition of the media, however, was so broad that it bordered on the eccentric. A medium, thought McLuhan, meant any extension of the human body – any kind of in-between or go-between connecting humans to the wider world, and anything that was designed to lend them power and speed, from the walking stick to the wheel. Whereas most previous social theorists, include Wiener and Brand, saw technology and media as tools to be used by humans for their own purposes, McLuhan preferred to think of them as having become so much a part of ourselves that it was difficult to know who was in control. 'We shape our tools,' said McLuhan, 'and thereafter they shape us.' So powerful had the modern media become, he argued, that we were no longer masters of our media technology but slaves (or 'servomechanisms') to its function. While McLuhan borrowed heavily from the ideas of Norbert Wiener, there were some important differences between the two. Wiener's theory had assumed the fundamental importance of messages in any system: that anything at all could be reduced to messages capable of being passed around an electronic information loop. McLuhan, on the other hand, affected to have no interest in messages at all. Instead, he spent much of his energy emphasising the importance of the medium or container through which those messages had been pushed. In 1965, McLuhan had coined his famous dictum – which became one of the most famous slogans of the twentieth century – 'the medium is the message.' The really important thing to be understood about any medium for communication, he insisted, was not what was being communicated but the change of pace or scale that the new medium introduced into society. The content of the medium was no more than a 'juicy piece of meat carried by the burglar to distract the watchdog of the mind'.

Marshall McLuhan's treatise on the influence of Gutenberg and his printing press was intriguing, but it was only ever intended as ammunition for his follow-up argument that the mechanical, book-based era was already on its way out. The rise of electrification and the shift from industrially produced, machine-like processes to the use of electrical circuits, he argued, was slowly linking human beings together on a global scale, and would eventually come to tie humanity together in unprecedented ways. As we moved further and further into the era of electrification and instant speed our media would become not only extensions of our body but extensions of our mind and our central nervous system too. We were on the cusp; McLuhan wanted to put everyone on notice of 'the final phase of the extensions of man – the technological simulation of consciousness, when the creative process of knowing will be collectively and corporately extended to the whole of society, much as we have already extended our senses and our nerves by the various media'. It was too early to decide how this simulation of consciousness in an electronic information loop would turn out, he admitted, but the effect would surely be to intensify our attachment to each other and to the conse-quences of our actions. With the ongoing development of the 'electric global network' everything from the factory to the nation-state would have to be either rethought or abandoned. The printing press had brought with it the idea for splitting up any production process into its constituent parts, each of which could then be placed one after another in an infinitely repeatable sequence of processes. The result was to inspire not only the factory assembly line, but the entire linear arrangement of modern society. 'The linearity precision and uniformity of the arrangement of movable types,' argued McLuhan, 'are inseparable from these great cultural forms and innovations of Renaissance experience.' Not only was the printing press the archetype of modern life, he continued, but so also were the books that it printed to order. Since people now tended to read privately, the humble book tended to accentuate the development of a fixed and private point of view. It was the first real teaching machine, had brought forth universal literacy and had given rise to a culture in which the visual act of reading came to take priority over the oral tradition that had flourished before it. Most importantly, said McLuhan, since each word followed on from another on the page and each page followed the previous one in the book, it had given rise to a world in which everything seemed to be uniform and continuous.

With the coming electrical age of speeded-up movement of information, however, McLuhan believed that all this was about to change. The mundane mechanical world of industry and machine production, as well as everything else, was about to be shocked into life by the passage of continuous, electrically driven streams of information through it. Information feedback loops like those that had been introduced into the operation of Wiener's anti-aircraft gun were about to be introduced into everyone and everything, and would eventually herald the demise of the linear approach to life that had taken its cue from the production of the book. As we shuffled our way from a world of mechanical sequences into one of dazzling electrification and instant speed, the new electric means of ferrying information around would alter our way of reading books just as surely as the printing press had modified the medieval practice of monks writing books by hand. That, however, was only the beginning of it. Where once just about everything had moved according to a one-way mechanical sequence of processes, McLuhan believed that we would now have to dance to the much faster rhythm of an electronic information loop linking everything to everything else all of the time. The machine age was dying and the new age of cybernetics was rising to take its place. The impact of this 'new electronic interdependence', thought McLuhan, might eventually restore the intimacy and community of tribal or medieval village life; with a little luck it might even precipitate the rise of a 'global village' and a new era of greater responsibility and understanding. Whereas the high priests of the counter-culture had seen the birth of a new kind of human consciousness in small-scale, village-like communities in which like-minded hippies could chat to one other, McLuhan saw it in an electronic village in which each individual would be tied, via electronic cables, to a shared global consciousness. This electric 'unified field of experience' would, because of its speed and its instantaneous ability to adjust itself to new information, look much like a collective brain.

Marshall McLuhan's enthusiasm for his 'global electrical network' was not simply a love of technology for its own sake. Indeed, one way of looking at his life and work is to see it as not a love affair with media technology but an epic spiritual adventure. Born into a devoutly religious family with Scottish-Irish roots, McLuhan had claimed the status of a conservative maverick even before he had reached adulthood. Throughout his career, from his days studying the Bible at university to his daredevil aphorisms about the modern media, McLuhan saw himself at war with the rational, mechanical, secular and materialist ideas that he had convinced himself were threatening to swamp the spiritual basis of modern life. As he drifted, while on a scholarship in Cambridge, from his childhood steeped in the Baptist religion towards a conversion to Catholicism, his own mother had chided him for his 'religion-hunting'. McLuhan's pressing need for a spiritual home leaked into his understanding of how electricity cables were about to change the world. 'Might not,' he wondered aloud in one of his books, 'our current translation of our entire lives into the spiritual form of information seem to make of the entire globe, and of the human family, a single consciousness?' Once all of our brains had been hooked up into a single global brain and our consciousness transferred into electronic information the warm glow of global electrical wholeness might lead to something truly transcendent.

By 1968, however, obsessed with the magnetism and the monolithic power of the broadcast media, McLuhan's mood had darkened. The coming electronic global village might not give rise to a village-like harmony after all, but precipitate a new kind of tribalism and conflict. He had begun to fear that television was exacerbating racial tensions in America, even going as far as to recommend a temporary ban on all television broadcasts in an effort to cool things down. McLuhan was also predicting a terrible economic depression that would arrive in five years' time and bring Western society to its knees. But as McLuhan's media-saturated vision lurched from utopia to apocalypse, his religious mysticism was only growing in its fervour. In a 1969 interview he came very close to arguing that the age of electronic media heralded nothing less than the Second Coming of Christ. 'Psychic communal integration made possible at last by the electronic media,' he told an astonished interviewer, 'could create the universality of consciousness foreseen by Dante when he predicted that men would continue as no more than broken fragments until they were unified into an inclusive consciousness. In a Christian sense, this is merely a new interpretation of the mystical body of Christ; and Christ, after all, is the ultimate extension of man.' For an academic and intellectual, it was an audacious thesis. Typically of McLuhan, his choice of medium was at least as interesting as the message. The interview appeared in the March issue of that august periodical, *Playboy* magazine.

Marshall McLuhan was not the only one worried about the power of the broadcast media at the end of the sixties. A new generation of activists and radical artists, as we saw in the last chapter, was mounting a fresh challenge to authority, and using the theories of both McLuhan and Wiener to do so. It wasn't long before some of them turned their attention to the most visible manifestation of the system: network television. Inspired by Wiener's vision of the perfect cybernetic society as one regulated by a generous helping of information feedback loops to improve its performance, some began to argue that the 'closed circuit' of broadcast television needed urgently to be smashed open so that ordinary people could join in the process. They made their point in a variety of ways. The winner of the award for most political film at the 1968 Vienna Film Festival was called *Ping Pong*, by Valie Export, and came with its own paddle and ball to be wielded by the viewer. The screen consisted of one half of a ping-pong table; black dots would appear on the screen and the viewer was supposed to whack the ball at them with the paddle as if engaged in a game of ping-pong with the film itself. At around the same time, activist artist and documentary groups in London and New York with names like Raindance, Videofreex and Global Village were mounting elaborate closed-circuit works of video art that did nothing more than film the audience and play the footage back to them. The idea behind experiments such as these was to strip away illusions about the power of television, reminding viewers that it had the potential to be a two-way process in which the audience could become a part of the network and feed back information as well as receive it. In 1970 a group of artists went as far as to establish a magazine called *Radical Software*, whose first issue's front cover announced the birth of something called the Radical Television Movement. At the end of each issue, in keeping with its cybernetic ethos, there was a section called 'Feedback' in which various video groups were invited to contribute whatever they liked as the results were pasted onto the page in no particular order.

This new coterie of technology activists borrowed the idea of information as feedback directly from Norbert Wiener, but what they meant by it was much more subversive and double-edged. Lifting the idea of feedback from engineering, Wiener had meant it to refer to the streams of information looped back or fed back into any system to improve or stabilise its operation. That, however, was not the only meaning of the word. If the information looped back into the system acted to reinforce the problem that it was intended to correct, it tended to disrupt the workings of a system rather than improve it. If left unchecked in a closed information loop, this 'bad' feedback (confusingly called 'positive feedback' by engineers) would only reinforce or amplify its errors and become unpleasant, noisy or dangerous. Think, for example, of what happens when a microphone is placed too close to a loud-speaker – the result is that the sound from the loudspeaker, or output, feeds back into the microphone, or input, giving rise to a screech or howl. Adding their own spin to Norbert Wiener's cybernetic information loop, the artists and bohemi-ans of the counter-culture thought they could make use of both kinds of feedback. Contemporary elites, they felt, were in dire need of receiving 'good' feedback from ordinary people, and the absence of that feedback was blighting the operation of society, just as Wiener had suggested it would. For these anti-authoritarian activists, however, there was always the suspicion that those in authority would pay no attention and trick people into thinking they were really making a difference by getting involved. It was at this point that the radicals would take out of their armoury a darker kind of feed-back with which to deliberately jam elite communication. One easy interpretation of this game of table tennis played between viewer and screen in *Ping Pong*, for example, was that it was an attempt to rouse viewers from their traditional pas-sivity as spectators and involve them in the action. But all was not as it first appeared: the artist saw it very differently. What she had created was a game whose direction was dictated entirely by the director and whose aim was to make people aware that their participation was being manipulated from above. Whacking balls back and forth at dots on a screen, those who played along with the film thought that they were deeply and actively involved in the information loop. The screen, however, wasn't playing ball. The appearance of the dots on the screen had been choreographed far in advance, and the players were being taken for fools.

This idea of 'culture jamming' eventually went on to become influential in its own right, but it was not the only concept to emerge from Wiener's theory of cybernetics. With generous funding from the American military, technology researchers were hard at work trying to build a new synthesis between man and electrical machine in its image. The invention of the computer mouse interface between man and computer by military-sponsored researchers in California in the sixties, for example, owed a huge debt to Norbert Wiener. The combination of mouse and on-screen cursor was modelled explicitly on Wiener's anti-aircraft predictor machine, and was designed to encourage a looping cycle of instruction and feedback so that users would learn the habit of constantly adjusting the position of their cursor by reacting to the evidence of its erratic movement across their computer screen. When I move an on-screen cursor when writing this chapter, for example, what I am doing is executing instructions with my hand while I observe the results of those actions a few centimetres away on the screen. In doing so, I am constantly closing the circle of an information feedback loop and thus maintaining the stability of the system and improving communication within it. On 9 December 1968, at a demonstration in San Francisco, a former navy radar technician called Douglas Engelbart unveiled this computer-mouse combination. Like an arrival from a more advanced planet, Engelbart showed a bamboozled audience how his mouse, in conjunction with an on-screen cursor, could be used to move information around and hop from one place to another. No one had seen anything like it, but even before it had been unveiled a young computer visionary called Ted Nelson, working at Brown University on a similar system for information retreival, had given it its own name: hypertext.

The technician holding the video camera during Engelbart's atmospheric demonstration of hypertext in 1968 was none other than Stewart Brand. Brand had taken a day off from putting together the *Whole Earth Catalog* to be part of Engelbart's production team. Like many mystical, hippie-influenced theories of the time, what Brand was ultimately looking for was a way to show that everything in the world was connected to everything else — some kind of proof that, as his former art-house associates at USCO had put it, 'we are all one'. What distinguished Brand from many other counter-cultural dreamers was that, in the *Whole Earth Catalog*, he had tried to find a way of bringing it about. The *Catalog*, however, had soon run its course. It had sold millions, but the enormous scale of its operation meant that it had been swallowed whole by the mainstream books trade and the mail order business. In any case, by the early seventies many of its subscribers had tired of communal living and were returning in their droves to San Francisco. Both they and Brand were badly in need of something that would further the cybernetic mission begun in the pages of the *Catalog*, a publishing medium reliable enough to allow peers to swap information between themselves outside of the purview of anyone else.

In the nascent computer industries that were springing up all over California they found exactly what they were looking for. In January 1968 there were fifty thousand computers operating in the whole of the country, of which fifteen thousand had been installed in the previous year. Their numbers were growing at an astounding rate; in the fifties, computer manufacturers had famously estimated that the whole of the United States was only in need of six computers. The appearance and public image of computers was changing too. Computers were no longer the sinister and forbidding contraptions of the post-war era, as big as a wardrobe and illuminated by the apparently random flashes of myriad buttons. They were getting more portable and more manageable. The development of these new computing machines owed more than a little to the ideas of Norbert Wiener. Even as Wiener was holding forth at conferences of the Cybernetics Group and decrying the abuses of his ideas by military research programmes, the military was making good use of cybernetic thinking to understand both its own activities and the uses of computers in general. For military engineers, cybernetics was useful because it helped weapons manufacturers to think of soldiers and their high-tech weaponry not as discrete elements within a battle plan but as fully integrated components of a single system whose operation was regulated by the ebb and flow of information in its component parts. The American military's SAGE (Semi-Automatic Ground Environment) air defence project, for example, was devised in the early fifties as an attempt to build an early warning system against Soviet bombers armed with nuclear weapons. Working from MIT, the very same university in which Wiener had worked to produce his own prototype of an anti-aircraft fire control machine during the Second World War, the team from SAGE was the first to build a working anti-aircraft system using cybernetics as a tool with which to model how information could course around a system and keep everything within it up-to-date. The project took over a decade to complete and cost more than a billion dollars. It was one of the biggest ever undertaken by the American military, and one of the first to take advantage of state-of-the art computing equipment.

Computers like those deployed in the SAGE early-warning system were built with much greater complexity than those that had gone before, and were gradually finding their feet as tools for communication as well as stand-alone number-crunching machines. By the early sixties, as Wiener's health had begun to deteriorate, the Pentagon had decided to try to harness the combined power of its computers and had asked its research arm – the Defense Advanced Research Projects Agency, otherwise known as DARPA – to investigate the possibilities. With money diverted directly from the American defence budget, teams of researchers began to construct what one of them dubbed an 'intergalactic network'. The result, called ARPANET, was the world's first-ever bank of computers, and was launched on 29 October 1969 when an interface that allowed the University of California at Los Angeles (UCLA) to communicate with Stanford University via computer terminals was built. The first message sent was 'LO' – it was supposed to have read 'LOGIN', but was accidentally abbreviated when the entire network of computers promptly crashed. By the end of the year, there were four nodes on ARPA's network: UCLA, Stanford University, the University of California at Santa Barbara and the University of Utah. Two years later the industrious researchers at ARPANET had managed to send the first ever e-mail, even if it was only passed to a computer in the next room.

Beyond the need for effective anti-aircraft missile systems, there were good reasons why the American military wanted to throw huge sums of money at research into personal computers and computer-based communication devices. In the late sixties, the Cold War with the Soviet Union and its satellite states was at its apogee, and had spilled over not only into an arms race but into an unseemly tussle over who could conquer the virgin terrain of space. Now that many media gurus such as Marshall McLuhan were predicting that machinery and heavy industry would shortly give way to a society based around the flow of information through a kind of global network, that race for technological superiority would have to be extended to computers. The Soviets and their allies had read their Norbert Wiener too, and not a few among them saw in 'cybernetic communism' an opportunity to make their flailing, command-and-control economies more efficient. In 1971, for example, the leftist government of Salvador Allende in Chile had inaugurated an innovative cybernetic system called Project Cybersyn as a way of extending Wiener's information loops into improving coordination among the different sectors of the Chilean economy. An English technology guru called Stafford Beer had been drafted in to implant what he called an 'electronic nervous system' deep in the Chilean economy, and early results were impressive.

Even as the Cold War heated up, however, governments did not have a monopoly on the race to build the first global electrical network. By the early seventies, Stewart Brand and his coterie of *Whole Earth Catalog* enthusiasts had stepped out from under the wreckage of the counter-culture with a new vigour and self-belief. While the culture jammers wanted to hijack broadcast television and open up its information loop to ordinary people, Stewart Brand had his own radical ideas about how to use a medium to further his radical agenda. Rumours of daring experiments in connecting people up using banks of computers were already filtering out from California's military research laboratories and university technology departments, and Brand – at the centre of so many different milieux, thanks to his work at the *Whole Earth Catalog* – was ideally placed to hear them. Many veterans of the counter-culture had by now turned into computer hobbyists, and were playing around with desktop-sized computer technology at home. Then there were the scientists and academics, many of whom had experimented in the counter-culture, after all, and were now looking for their own way of using technology to make the world a better place. By 1972, Brand was even bold enough to argue that computers were the natural successor to LSD. Like the newest hippie drug, they were a small-scale and highly portable technology that might be used to open minds to new, more progressive ways of thinking.

In the course of the seventies, as computers became more prevalent both Marshall McLuhan and Stewart Brand could consider their ideas somewhat vindicated. It was McLuhan, after all, who had made it his life's work to argue that the machinery of the industrial age was in the throes of giving way to a global electronic network. Influenced by McLuhan's work, Brand had, by the beginning of the decade, had a similar epiphany. There was no denying that his friends in the counter-culture had failed miserably in building a shared consciousness and promoting a more egalitarian society by simply retreating into communes. Armed with computers and a means of hooking them up to each other, Brand began to think that he might have more luck.

The two men make for an instructive comparison, if only because they seem very far from natural bedfellows. The chasm between McLuhan and the pranksters and provocateurs of the counter-culture, as embodied by Brand, narrows as soon as one takes into account their reference points and the directions

from which they were coming. For one thing, both McLuhan
and Brand had been deeply and formatively influenced by the
cybernetics of Norbert Wiener and his ideas about how
humans could benefit from being tied together in a continuous
information loop of instruction and feedback. Then there was
the question of belief. McLuhan, as we have seen, was a man of
strong and deeply felt religious convictions who saw in his
electrical network nothing less than an opportunity to bring
human beings closer together in a new kind of divine revelation. Brand was not religious in the conventional sense. Ever
since he graduated from Stanford in 1960 he had been both a
seeker and a spiritual dilettante. Both McLuhan and Brand
were badly in need of something that might give practical
expression to their spiritual convictions. As it turned out, they
chose the same thing.

But what was it that both McLuhan and the hippies came to
believe in, other than a dense thicket of cables threaded
together with computers like lights on some gigantic
Christmas tree? For McLuhan the birth of this new electronic
medium held out the prospect of pooling our human consciousness in a single global brain or global village. At the
same time, but for different reasons, the rapidly advancing
technology of computerisation came as a godsend to many
hippies and former commune-dwellers. The key tenet of the
counter-culture's intellectual heavyweights was that everything on earth was tied to everything else in an organic
whole – that if only people were put into direct communication with their peers outside of the reach of central authority
they could enhance this sense of a shared human consciousness
and tune into something beyond their immediate selves. For
both McLuhan the religious mystic and the electro-hippies, the

communications tie became, quite literally, the missing spiritual link that could renew their faith and their sense of purpose. If this was a vision of a new universal consciousness, it was one tied together not by God or by Gaia, but by an electrical circuit.

This new kind of electronic tie linking everyone to everyone else in a global village would be quite different to the ties that people had relied on before. It would not be built around shared proximity or shared geography, or even shared values, but on shared access to electronic information. This revelation about the overriding importance of an electronic medium came in different ways to Marshall McLuhan and Stewart Brand. McLuhan summarised it in his emphatic insistence that the medium was the message; that insufficient attention had hitherto been paid to the transforming power of media extensions which anchored us to the rest of the world. For Brand and his fellow new media activists, it arrived along with the realisation that it was better to bring people together in direct communication rather than to prescribe what they might want to hear. What was going to matter above all in the coming global village was the electronic medium that connected people. Everything else had to be stripped back or thrown out. If this new kind of electronic tie was to be the foundation of a global village, it could only do so by remaining oblivious to those messy aspects of human identity and society – race, gender and politics, for example – that were only incidental to its operation.

McLuhan's prognostications now look satisfyingly prescient, even if they didn't turn out quite how he imagined. Given how the internet has subsequently developed into a constantly shifting mass of information built and navigated by ordinary people, his extravagant cybernetic vision now seems much more credible. His aphorism that the medium is the message, too, was richer and more eerily prophetic than he could ever have imagined. Though McLuhan didn't live to see it, messages sent via our electronic links on texts, e-mails and online social networks are rapidly becoming our medium of choice. If McLuhan was right that the content of our media is often less important than the containers in which it is housed, then we can expect that the time that we spend ceaselessly passing information back and forth between our electronic ties might also reverberate throughout our culture in subtle and often unacknowledged ways.

The fascination of Marshall McLuhan and the electro-hippies with the medium over its message left one final legacy. In the late sixties and early seventies the ideas of McLuhan and Brand were only of marginal interest, and discussion of their cybernetic theories barely rippled beyond bohemians and modish intellectuals. When the technology that they championed was made accessible to everyone, and electronic ties gave rise to networks thick with connections, their overarching concern with the medium through which information is pushed, rather than its content or its purpose, would itself begin to seem much more plausible, and to affect how we think about who we are. If our new electronic medium was so important a measure of us, then it would become tempting to reduce everything we touched to a network of ties. Rather like those over-enthusiastic MIT researchers in the nineties, whose insistence on weighing themselves down with electronic gizmos distracted them from what they hoped to achieve, there was always the danger that the medium would overwhelm the message.

For these breathless new believers in the power of the electronic tie, none of this mattered. Our new electronic connections, they felt sure, were going to propel us into a higher state of communion, a truly universal consciousness in which we would no longer have much need of our bodily selves. To the architects of Cyburbia, what we were talking about or where we were headed counted for little because, tethered to each other via a shiny new electronic medium, everyone was going to be in constant communication with everyone else.

4

The Network Effect

In 2007 Pierre Bayard, a professor of French literature at the University of Paris, wrote a book arguing that reading books from cover to cover was a waste of time. The book became a surprise best-seller in France, and was subsequently translated into English under the title *How To Talk About Books You Haven't Read*. In it Bayard readily admitted that he often talks to students about books he hasn't read; his students, he suggested, might think about doing the same. Room could even be found in the curriculum for a course inculcating the art of not reading books, and the knack of talking about them anyway.

How To Talk About Books You Haven't Read set the literary world ablaze. Outraged, many critics panned it; in an effort to wind its author up, some even wrote about it without reading it. Bayard's book may have sounded like a charter for bluffers and literary charlatans but it was more sophisticated than it looked. His thesis was that non-reading – which, for him, included skimming books and flightily dipping in and out of them – was a new and increasingly common engagement with the literary canon, and just as respectable as reading books. More important than mere books, reckoned Bayard, were the teeming associations that tied those books together in the literary 'system'. Given that none of us has the time or the patience to read everything, it might be better just to imbibe a general sense of what was out there – to get ourselves a rough idea of what books were about and where they fitted in relation to other books in the virtual library. We forget most of what we read, and only remember fragments of books, which ceaselessly mix themselves up in our imagination. It would save us a good deal of trouble if we didn't bother with them at all.

For Pierre Bayard, books had ceased to be objects in their own right. From now on they would be defined solely by their relationships with other books. Decades after Marshall McLuhan predicted the demise of the book-based era, one way of looking at the trick that Bayard had performed was that he had shattered the book as a medium and replaced it with a newer kind of medium, one based not in bound bits of paper and cloth but on the shifting and manifold ties and associations that can be drawn between books as a system. Enthusiasts for this new medium, following McLuhan's lead, had little interest in things in themselves. Instead they boasted a forensic determination to map the web of relationships in which those objects were embedded. For the most part, they called themselves network theorists.

Network theory is not just a way to talk about books. It has been making inroads into the understanding of us humans for some time. Social network theory is generally dated from

1967, when a Harvard social psychologist called Stanley Milgram, intrigued by the urban legend that anyone can put themselves in touch with anyone else by tapping their friends and their friends' friends in only a small number of easy hops, decided to conduct a series of unusual sociological experiments. He started by having letters sent to a few hundred randomly selected people in Boston and Omaha, asking their recipients to send them on to a stockbroker who worked in a small town called Sharon in Massachusetts. There were, however, very strict rules. Recipients of the letters were given a great deal of information about the stockbroker, but were only allowed to send their letters via friends and acquaintances and not simply by posting them directly to him. The idea was that each would forward their letters to someone more likely to know the stockbroker until the letter arrived safely in his hands. Milgram's answer to the question of how many hands the letters would, on average, have to pass through before they arrived at their destination was only six, and his study was forever after known as the small-world experiment. His attention-grabbing conclusions quickly filtered their way through into popular culture, and were immortalised in John Guare's 1990 play, *Six Degrees of Separation*. The world, Milgram's experiment seemed to prove, really was a small and densely connected place.

Stanley Milgram's study made for an entertaining parlour game, but it also spurred other academics to think about applying the idea of networks to understanding society. For some time a minority of social scientists had been thinking about people as information processors and society as a giant computer network, with messages passed around from one tie to another courtesy of the bountiful connections made possible by that network. To many of its critics, social network theory sounded trite and obvious, but the claims it made were really quite distinctive. Whereas other social scientists worked by imagining society either as a collection of atomised individuals or as a lifeless structural glue, social network theorists stood back to take a bird's-eye view of the social landscape and then carefully mapped the web of relationships that seemed to make it up. They claimed that it would rapidly become apparent that society was composed of many different overlapping groups because the people within them could be found to have multiple different ties and affiliations. The metaphor of networks was initially borrowed from communication infrastructures such as the telephone system, where a network was simply a means of communication made out of nodes or sockets and the connections between them. For social network theorists, humans could be seen as analogous to the nodes on these electronic communications systems, and the ties they formed were very much like electronic connections. Add up all those ties or connections and the result was a network just like any other.

The unusual thing about networks for communication, however, is that they refuse to add up in a straightforward, linear fashion. Imagine that you buy two walkie-talkies for your home, so that you and your spouse can speak to each other in different parts of the house. When you talk to your spouse using one of those walkie-talkies, you need only one connection to link up the two. Continue to imagine, however, that you go back to the shop and buy another so that one of your children can tune in too. This proves an excellent idea. Now you can use your walkie-talkie to talk to your partner; your partner can use it to talk to your son; and your son can use it to talk to you. By buying just one more walkie-talkie you've tripled the number of possible connections. Now imagine that your daughter wants to use the system too, and so you acquiesce and buy one for her as well. When you and the rest of your family start using the four walkie-talkies that you now own, you find that there are three novel ways to use them and a total of six connections; your daughter can talk to you, she can talk to your partner, and she can also use her walkie-talkie to chat with her brother. And so on, with the number of connections increasing steeply as you shell out for more and more walkie-talkies for your extended family.

This irreducible truth – that the value of a communications system rises much faster than the number of units of which it is made up – is known to technology enthusiasts as the network effect. There are a number of different mathematical ways of presenting it, and much dispute about the precise formula, but all have in common the idea that the number of possible ties or connections between nodes on a network rises much faster than the number of nodes themselves. If we were to plot that growth along the vertical axis of a graph, we would find that it rises not in a straight line but in a sharply nonlinear upwards swoop. A good way to imagine it is to consider the market for fax machines. A single fax machine is no use at all, since there is no one to fax. However, as soon as everyone else gets one fax machines can be very useful indeed. Making any given network bigger brings vast advantages because the rapidly growing number of connections between those who are on it creates its own momentum. As the number of nodes on a network grows, they criss-cross each other so quickly as to make a rainbow of different connections, and this explosion of fresh ties makes the network infinitely more powerful than it would otherwise have been. The system generates network effects.

The idea of networks intrigued a few academics in the late sixties and early seventies, but the truth was that the idea of applying it to society would never have taken off if their enthusiasm had not been shared by a movement armed with a new technology. The academic social network theorists and the hippie new communications technology enthusiasts had much in common. Just as the electronic ties or connections between people had begun to assume an almost ethereal importance for veterans of the counter-culture such as Stewart Brand, the defining feature of social network theory was that it wasn't at all interested in people as individuals but only in the relationships that held them together. More than that, and again in common with the motley gurus of cybernetics, social network theorists were really only interested in humans as the efficient senders and receivers of information, and how messages could hop from one place to another in the network. It was here, within this dense network of informational ties, that the social network theorists thought they could locate the essence of society, and the secret of social change.

While the network theorists were talking up social networks, what remained of the counter-culture was hard at work building them. As the seventies progressed computers shrunk to the size of desktops and companies building them grew up around the San Francisco Bay Area. The hippies who had migrated to communes in the hills surrounding San Francisco in the late sixties were now back in town, and were keen to get involved in the nascent computer industry and lend it a degree

of counter-cultural cool. As hippies morphed into electro-hippies, San Francisco and the areas around it became a haven for
an alternative community of computer hackers and programmers in the same way that it had been for bohemians years
before. Computers with microprocessors small enough to be
used in the home began to appear in the middle of the seventies, and in 1981 the American technology giant IBM began to
manufacture these new personal computers in huge quantities.
Two years later, Stewart Brand was hawking around a successor to the *Whole Earth Catalog* called the *Whole Earth
Software Catalog*, whose aim was to spread the word about
the new personal computers just as the original *Catalog* had
spread the word about alternative living. The following year,
in 1984, the manifesto of the new movement was televised in
the form of the California-based Apple Computer Inc.'s famous
advertisement for its Macintosh personal computer. Apple's
ad, one of the most enduring and influential of all time, was
directed by Ridley Scott and featured an athletic and not-at-all-
geeky blonde racing past the seated masses at a sinister-looking
rally to throw a hammer at the Orwellian Big Brother figure
whose image appeared on a giant screen. Freedom was on
its way, the ad suggested, and it could be coming to a desktop near you if only you bought yourself an Apple personal
computer.

What really attracted the hippies to the computer industry
was not so much the computers themselves but the possibility
of using them to allow people to talk to their peers outside of
the reach of either authority or hierarchy. To Norbert Wiener's
image of humans as highly responsive steersmen living their
lives in a never-ending loop of information, the modern disciples of cybernetics had added their own twist. What the

veterans of the communes wanted was nothing less than to make these new computer networks human – to turn them into networks of activist nodes and allow the myriad electronic ties between us to flourish into a new kind of egalitarian community. The future looked to be on their side. In 1970, only a year after the first message was sent from computer to computer under the supervision of the American military, the system of interlinked computers had spread to thirteen different research centres; four years later, that number had leaped to fifty-seven. Helped along by computer hobbyists and the resources of university computer science departments, this early network of computers was cobbled together, with computers being added to the network only as the need seemed to arise. A decade later computer networking had grown up enough that it was ready to leave the universities and military think-tanks and, in 1985, it was no surprise to those who knew him to learn that Stewart Brand had decided to establish a community-based network in the San Francisco Bay Area.

The WELL, the acronym by which Brand's Whole Earth 'Lectronic Link became known, was a rough-and-ready version of the internet that allowed its members to dial up a central computer server and type messages to each other whenever and about whatever they liked. It wasn't the only primitive computer-based communication machine to have appeared at the beginning of the eighties. Three years earlier, a weighty black-and-white computer terminal called the Minitel had been loaned (yes, loaned) to millions of French telephone users by PTT, the country's leading phone company, and many French people were taking the opportunity to type messages to each other at their leisure. What set the WELL apart from the Minitel were its distinctive ethos and the hugely influential

nature of its membership. In its inner circle were many of the
same Bay Area engineers, boffins and programmers who had
built the computers that were linked up to the WELL. Joining
them were journalists, musicians and what remained of the
counter-culture: a large proportion of early WELL users were
Deadheads, the legendarily loyal fans of the Grateful Dead.
Together they set about reinventing the same hippie sensibility fostered by the *Whole Earth Catalog* for a new kind of
electronic community. Brand based the architecture of the
WELL very deliberately on the cybernetic principles of his
earlier publishing experiment, and the *Catalog*'s egalitarian
sensibility showed heavily in the architecture of the WELL.
Most of the content on its bulletin boards was penned by its
members, and was in turn corrected and edited by other members. Over twenty years after the demise of the *Catalog*, Brand
would argue that his interest in self-sustaining networks for
egalitarian communication had been fully formed by the time
he had set it up in 1968. 'I set in motion a thing,' he told a
journalist from the *Los Angeles Times*, 'by which by purveying
the stuff, and being a node on a network of people purveying
it to each other . . . I would get to learn whatever that network
was learning . . . and it was designed as a system. I know about
systems. I had studied cybernetics.'

The politics of the counter-culture had long been eclipsed,
but its central idea of bringing about direct communication
between peers outside the reach of authority had survived
intact. If a new global consciousness could not be forged by
heading for the hills, Brand and his comrades at the WELL
reasoned, it would stand a much better chance of success when
it was fired by electronic communication rather than small-
scale communal living. The aim was to make the electronic

ties that they had begun to hold in such high regard coalesce in a network and give rise to a thousand blooming new connections. What they wanted was nothing less than to give human communication network effects.

As the high-tech economy of the San Francisco Bay Area spread outwards in the eighties and early nineties, and computers began to appear in more and more homes and offices, the idea of networks was quietly borrowed by economists and business leaders. While the computer industry seemed to be advancing in leaps and bounds, it helped that the old way of doing things – the traditional Fordist economy of manufacturing goods on strictly regimented factory assembly lines – was limping from recession to recession and that businesses, in the aftermath of huge and socially bruising layoffs in the eighties, were thirsting for new ideas. It occurred to many business thinkers that what they were witnessing were the birth pangs of a whole new economy, one thoroughly networked and constantly adjusting to the continuous feedback of its suppliers and its consumers. This new kind of economy would be powered by computers and electronic networking devices, to be sure, but it was about much more than just technology. What it demanded was nothing less than the levelling of the old-fashioned, hierarchical firm into a new, leaner kind of organisation that sat like a spider alongside its many and shifting employees and suppliers like a node in a network. In the coming networked world, it was forecast by breathless management gurus and technology boosters, organisations were going to become leaderless and it was going to be vitally important to cultivate relationships with one's extended network. Articles appeared in the *Harvard Business Review*, for example, to argue that the kind of companies that grow and expand are those which place at least as much emphasis on their relationships with other firms and their customers as on what they produce. Work and leadership were slowly giving way to network, who you knew was becoming at least as important as what you did.

The band of merry veterans around Stewart Brand were happy to play their part in spreading the word about the power of networks. In fact, many of them went on to become cheerleaders and evangelists for the new, networked approach to business organisation. In 1987 Brand was given a job as a visiting fellow at MIT's prestigious Media Lab. In his history of the university's involvement in communications technology that was published in the same year, *The Media Lab: Inventing the Future at MIT*, he was moved to argue that the Media Lab was a direct descendant of the laboratory at MIT in which Norbert Wiener had laboured to invent cybernetic principles nearly half a century earlier. Also in the same year, Brand and some friends set up the Global Business Network or GBN, a consulting firm that made it its mission to advise top global companies on how to adapt their hierarchical monoliths to the flexible, networked future. Like the *Whole Earth Catalog*, the GBN took its cue from a heady mix of cybernetics and the hippie loathing of institutional hierarchies, and excited a new generation of executives with its radical chic and its understanding of how they could change around their organisations in order to adapt to a fast-changing world. In January 1993 a new magazine was launched in San Francisco by Kevin Kelly, a long-time associate of Brand and a former editor of the *Whole Earth Catalog*. *Wired* was to play a crucial role as pied piper to the whole idea of the new economy. In its launch issue it was already claiming Marshall McLuhan as its patron saint and looking forward to a world of ubiquitous computer devices all seamlessly connected in a giant global network – strictly egalitarian, perfectly self-organising and utterly free from authority.

By the nineties, the computer metaphor championed by Wiener as a way of understanding how humans behave had been refined and extended into the network metaphor, and it was slowly extending its reach into the rest of the economy. Huge multinational companies began re-engineering their operations according to cybernetic principles. Between the sixties and the nineties, one study of management literature in Western countries by two French sociologists found, the number of mentions of networks increased more than twentyfold. After all, the logic went, if something as flat as a network could be so powerful, why not stretch everything into the same, perfectly flat shape? Hierarchies were firmly out, and were everywhere being granulated into small teams of human nodes who could be more adaptable and responsive to a constant stream of information from their extended information network. Managers were no longer strictly required to manage, but to build networks of relationships that they could keep at their fingertips and take with them whenever they moved on. Neither were they supposed to remain entirely in control. The only way that the art of management could survive in the networked world, suggested Kevin Kelly in his 1995 book *Out of Control*, was to relinquish control and let people organise themselves. In all the ritual denunciations of hierarchy and bureaucracy it wasn't hard to see the influence of former hippies and leftists, who had spent 1968 criticising faceless bureaucrats and labyrinthine hierarchies and were now, in comfortable middle age, more than happy to bring those same institutions down to size. Neither was it difficult to see the hand of Norbert Wiener. Indeed, Kevin Kelly informed his readers that his book was no more than 'an update on the current state of cybernetic research'. By 1998, Kelly was offering even more ambitious updates. Writing in a magazine called the *Whole Earth Review* in 1998, a successor to Brand's *Whole Earth Catalog*, Kelly claimed to have discovered that 'the universe is a computer', and that the idea of computer networks would soon help to explain life, the universe and everything. It was, he gushed, 'a new universal metaphor. It has more juice in it than previous metaphors: Freud's dream state, Darwin's variety, Marx's progress, or the Age of Aquarius. And it has more power than anything else in science at the moment. In fact the computational metaphor may eclipse mathematics as a form of universal notation.'

What made the computer network metaphor all the more attractive as the twentieth century drew to a close was the acknowledged truth of the network effect as it applied to the power of communications equipment. The network effect became such a talking point that it was invoked in speeches by both President Bill Clinton and his deputy Al Gore. Gore was no stranger to high-tech futurology. For some years before his commencement address in 1996 he had been talking up, in luridly utopian terminology, the building of an 'information highway' and the building of a vast fibre-optic telecommunications network to bring about fast broadband access to the internet. Since this new infrastructure was going to link everyone together, stock analysts and high-tech gurus agreed, its construction contained network effects and its value was bound to rise far faster than the costs associated with putting it into the ground. Investors, as a consequence, no longer needed to heed either the business cycle or the conventional economic laws of profit and loss because both had been overturned by the network effect. All that was required was that they hunker down and wait until new technology companies had acquired their own self-sustaining momentum – and then reap the rewards. By July 1997 the cover story of *Wired* was forecasting 'THE LONG BOOM'. The article, co-authored by Peter Schwartz of the Global Business Network, teased its readers with the confident prediction that 'we're facing 25 years of prosperity, freedom and a better environment for the whole world. You got a problem with that?'

Virtually no one did. Determined not to be left out, many social scientists began to think that there might be something for them in the network metaphor too. New thinking purported to show that information as it was seen to pass through networks was central to understanding how society worked. In the early seventies, shortly after Stanley Milgram's small-world experiment, an American sociologist called Mark Granovetter had compared attempts by two different Boston neighbourhoods to mobilise themselves against threats from developers and had found vastly different results. In search of an answer as to why this was, Granovetter drew a map of the different connections among both sets of activists. It wasn't the strong and intense relationships forged between friends and workmates that proved the most effective spur to this kind of community activism, he discovered, but the presence of weak ties between casual acquaintances who had much less in common. The advantage of having a sprinkling of weak ties within an information network, according to Granovetter, lay in the rapidity with which information could then be transmitted from one place to another. Before long he was applying the same logic to the task of finding a job. Of much greater use than one's close friends when it comes to job hunting, Granovetter argued, were encounters with loose acquaintances. Since people from different walks of life were privy to different kinds of information from you and your friends they were more likely to be able to offer tips on which jobs were up for grabs.

Mark Granovetter's argument was that, just like the books on Pierre Bayard's bookshelf, people were often more usefully skimmed – encountered lightly but in greater numbers. Granovetter wasn't denying that strong ties could help people fortify their identities and oil the wheels of community life. His point was that communities and networks are very different things, and that just as communities need to be knitted together with strong ties, weak ties made between far-away nodes are equally important because they help information circulate to places which it otherwise would not be likely to reach. He was not alone in this view. By the late eighties and early nineties, when the bonds of traditional communities seemed to be fraying, some American sociologists claimed that it had simply given way to an amorphous phenomenon called networked individualism – a loose and shifting series of ties and affiliations that connected modern city-dwellers to those around them. It was around this time that the idea of networks finally leapt into the popular imagination. The humble circle of friends, for example, was overthrown in favour of the infinitely more glamorous extended network of friends and acquaintances.

French social theorists, meanwhile, were rushing to embrace social network theory because of their enthusiasm for the network principle that entities were best described not via their

ingrained characteristics but in terms of their constantly shifting relationships with those around them. In 1988 Bruno
Latour, a French sociologist of medicine, published *The
Pasteurization of France*, which argued that Louis Pasteur, the
celebrated nineteenth century inventor of pasteurisation, was
better seen not as an individual but as part of a vast network of
scientific colleagues, laboratories, scientific bacteria, notebooks, statistics and a prevailing atmosphere of colonial
racism. Louis Pasteur the diligent lone researcher, Latour
assured his readers, did not exist.

The network effect won over many in the late nineties, but it
didn't impress everyone. Some influential economists pointed
out that while computers and the internet had transformed
office life they had not had the revolutionary effect that the
technology boosters claimed. 'You can see the computer age
everywhere these days,' said the Nobel laureate in economics
Robert Solow drily, 'except in the productivity statistics.'
Neither did the propagandists for extending the network
metaphor have it all their own way. For many sociologists it
wasn't at all clear why labelling everything as a network added
anything to social investigation. A decade after the publication
of his celebrated book about Louis Pasteur, for example, Bruno
Latour had had enough. 'There are four things that do not
work with actor-network theory,' he told a confused workshop
of eager young French sociologists in 1997. 'The word actor,
the word network, the word theory and the hyphen. Four nails
in the coffin.' In the same year the American sociologist
Ronald Burt pointedly observed of the social network theorists
that 'their eyes go shifty like a cornered ferret if you push past
the network metaphor for details about how specific kinds of

relations matter'. A few economists even piped up to quibble about the insidious effect of the idea of networks on the world of work. With her tongue only partly in her cheek, Corinne Maier wrote a book called *Bonjour Paresse* ('Hello Laziness') in which she argued that old-fashioned work had become a waste of time because it no longer reaped any rewards. All, however, was not lost: 'Spend some time "selling yourself" and "networking",' Maier advised her readers, 'so that you have some back-up with which to protect yourself next time the company restructures.'

There was no doubt that the sceptics were on to something. The network theorists hadn't really explained, for example, why a theory aimed at understanding how computers could communicate with one another could be a reliable guide to human behaviour. For some businesses and professions, chiefly those in the media, it was obvious that diligent networking could pay dividends. For most people, however, paying too much attention to cultivating a network could prove a meaningless distraction. In addition, the determination of social network theorists to tie everything together could sometimes create as many problems as it helped solve. Thirty-five years after the findings of the breakthrough small world experiment had been published, a professor of psychology and fan of Stanley Milgram's work called Judith Kleinfeld decided to try to reproduce it for her students using e-mail rather than letters. To see how it was done, Kleinfeld travelled from her home in Alaska to the Yale University Library, which housed Milgram's private papers. What she found shocked her. In Milgram's initial attempt to get his experiment off the ground, only three of his sixty letters ever made it to their destination. Two other attempts were discreetly binned because response rates were so low. Even in later experiments, only 30 per cent of the letters arrived with their intended recipient. Milgram, she discovered, simply chose to exclude the vast majority of uncompleted chains from his analysis. Just as damning was her discovery that the studies which had tried to reproduce Milgram's findings, and which had been sent to him for his inspection, had all failed miserably.

Stanley Milgram so wanted it to be true that each of us are only six degrees of separation away from everyone else that he swept contradictory data right under the carpet. Writing in the late sixties, at a time when hippie visionaries were arguing that everything in the world was connected to everything else in an invisible, semi-mystical spiritual communion, perhaps he could be sure that his small world experiment would find an appreciative audience. The weak ties that appeared to hold us all together, however, were no more than the intellectual equivalent of an urban myth.

Dissident voices about the power of social networks, however, were never more than a minority view. With its promise of levelling hierarchies and laying bare hidden connections, the computer network metaphor was on the rise almost everywhere in the West. Norbert Wiener's cybernetic idea about the centrality of messages in motivating human action had travelled far, soaring upwards from the military-industrial establishment to the counter-culture, and from there into the business world and the rest of society. For some people, however, all this was not going to be enough. During the eighties and nineties, what had inspired politicians and technology gurus was the dream of connecting people up to an 'information highway' via underground cables. Humans were being tied to one another, to be sure, but the self-sustaining momentum of the network effect only applied to the fibre-optic cables that were being laid in the ground so that we could have lightning new broadband connections to the internet. As far as it applied to the humans on the receiving end of those cables, the network was still nothing more than an awkward metaphor. Even more insulting was that many of the people involved in laying the infrastructure for the information highway still persisted in seeing it as a one-way communication medium: a successor to television that would bring fresh opportunities for driving advertising, marketing and trade in their direction.

For the most radical disciples of cybernetics that was never really the point. What they wanted was nothing less than to push past the network metaphor and make it a reality, to weld themselves so directly to the computer network that the network effect — the ability of a network of nodes to transmit information between themselves and to tie each other up in a web of connections — could be made to apply not just to computers and cabling but to humans too. This idea of making the computer metaphor real had long been the stuff of cybernetic lore. It had also come a long way since Norbert Wiener had insisted that human beings were essentially messengers who were constantly adapting themselves to a continuous information loop.

It was soon to go even further. In 1990 an English computer scientist working in Geneva called Tim Berners-Lee brought the idea of a global information network a step closer when he developed the hypertext method of navigating through electronic information pioneered by Douglas Engelbart and Ted Nelson into a whole new system for browsing information on the internet. It became known as the world wide web, and within a few years it was to become everyone's first port of call when they connected to the internet. By the late nineties, however, there were plenty of signs that people were tiring of the one-way flow of information from websites and that they wanted to be more intimately involved in the information loop. Films like *The Truman Show* played with the public's appetite for seeing the lives of ordinary people reflected back to them on broadcast television networks. TV franchises like *Big Brother*, which was first aired in the Netherlands in 1999 and went on to become a genre-defining hit, attracted audiences of millions for shows that used CCTV cameras to broadcast a continuous feed of a group of ordinary people trying to go about their business. Such shows, of course, were tightly edited artifices created by professional television producers. Given the choice many of us have opted for the real thing, of peering right into someone's living room. At the beginning of 2006 I visited a brand new high-tech project called Shoreditch Digital Bridge in east London, whose purpose was to bring to two socially impoverished urban estates access to broadband and digital television, which their residents might not otherwise be able to afford. Almost as an afterthought the architects of the Shoreditch project had decided to offer residents access to images from a range of CCTV cameras that monitored the communal areas of their estates. In preliminary discussions with the residents, the manager of the project told me, none of them were remotely bothered by the implications for their privacy. Most, in fact, were highly enthusiastic. Some justified their interest in the CCTV as a crime prevention measure, but others admitted to a more prosaic reason for wanting to be surrounded by cameras – simple curiosity. They weren't kidding. By November 2007, according to a leaked internal report commissioned by local government, viewing figures for the scheme were as good as that for prime-time, weekday broadcast television. More people had tuned in to watch each other on CCTV than had bothered to watch *Big Brother*.

In retrospect, the alliances forged between CCTV and broadcast television seem like a fuzzy prototype for a world in which many of us would prefer to spend our leisure time hooked up to places on the internet where we could ogle our peers. In the late sixties, as we saw in the last chapter, new media activists had campaigned to break open the closed circuit of network television so that ordinary viewers could become senders of information as well as its passive receivers. Now their ideas were at last becoming a reality, but in a form that they could barely have imagined. For its watchers, perusing unvarnished humanity via peer-to-peer CCTV must be a little like staring at a documentary about wildlife in the savannah: one of those in which apparently bored animals wander into the gaze of the camera, scratch themselves listlessly and then shuffle off in search of something better to do. At one of the offices where I used to work, the receptionist had as her screensaver a live video image of wild animals lying around in a zoo cage. On a screen above her head she was able to look at images from a bank of CCTV cameras of the whole building. Darting from one to the other she must have discovered some similarities between the two.

The era in which we could become more intimately a part of the network, long predicted by media prophets such as Marshall McLuhan and worked towards by cybernetic agitators like Stewart Brand, was almost upon us. The prize was a place in which humans could be something more than day-tripping users of a high-tech panoply of cables and tie themselves more intimately into the medium. The promise was to extend the network effect into something more human: to render us capable of forging connections and passing information back and forth between those connections with all the ease and rapidity of nodes on a network. The irony is that it would take the calamitous humbling of one version of the network idea to ease the path of its second, more militant iteration. In 1999 Peter Schwartz, co-founder of the Global Business Network and co-author of 'The Long Boom', the article published in *Wired* several years earlier, produced a full-length book of the same name in which he detailed the coming age of unprecedented, technology-fuelled prosperity. The Long Boom was briefly fêted, but by the following year it was looking a trifle mouldy. In March 2000 the giddy rise of the market for high-technology stocks, puffed up with hot air about how the network effect was going to redefine the conventional laws of profit and loss, suddenly began to sink back to earth. A devastating controlled explosion in the high-tech economy followed, sweeping away the idea of the information highway and all those expensive and gimmicky websites that attracted huge amounts of investment but were good for very little.

Out of those ruins would emerge a more authentic expression of the original cybernetic idea, amid a spontaneous mass migration to Cyburbia.

5

Peer Pressure

If San Francisco in 1967 will forever be remembered as the Summer of Love, 2007 in London was most definitely the summer of promiscuous friendship on Facebook. In the space of only two months, Facebook.com exploded into a kind of electronic ectoplasm that found its sticky way into the life of almost every organisation, every dinner party anecdote, every budding romance. In the febrile atmosphere that followed, every conversation seemed to be punctuated with gambits like, 'How many friends do you have on Facebook?', 'I'll friend you on Facebook' or the slightly more ominous 'Consider yourself poked.'

Facebook was only three years old. One of the new generation of social networking sites populated by ordinary users sharing material produced by their peers – places like MySpace, YouTube and Second Life – the site was the brainchild of a Harvard undergraduate called Mark Zuckerberg who, at the age of nineteen, decided that the printed directory of mugshots which were issued to students at the beginning of term could do with being transferred online. Within a single day of its launch in February 2004, over a thousand of Zuckerberg's fellow students had signed up. From there Zuckerberg successfully exported the idea to other American universities, and then to universities and colleges around the world. It helped that signing up took no more than a couple of minutes. After that, new arrivals were encouraged to search for other people's profiles to see if there was anyone they could invite to be their Facebook 'friend'. The kind of friendship offered and usually accepted on Facebook is the glue that holds the place together. The blossoming of millions of new friendships adds bricks and mortar to the place; it helps thicken it with groups of people who can claim some kind of connection with one another. With a healthy stock of friends in their network, Facebookers could go on to use the 'status updates' function to broadcast news of their movements and see how everyone else was updating theirs. Most preferred to update their profiles with enigmatic, teasing and deliberately insubstantial little nuggets like 'Emma is feeling nauseous' and 'James is contemplating lunch' or, my favourite, 'Will is wondering how that car alarm would like it if he kicked it to death.' Then there was the poke, Facebook's signature function, a kind of electronic 'wassup' which Facebookers liked to send to friends and acquaintances just for fun.

Facebook wasn't the only online social networking site that thought of itself as the new new thing. It wasn't even the biggest. All the same, 2007 was undoubtedly the year in which it arrived in polite society, and no more so than in London. By July of that year 882,000 Londoners had pitched up there, double the number who were signed up just two months previously, and London overtook Toronto to become the biggest network on Facebook's system. With Europe now in its reach, Facebook was making inroads into the rest of the world. In the single month of May 2007 the number of Facebookers in South Africa doubled. Even in India, where it was dwarfed by another social networking site called Orkut, its membership tripled in the first six months of 2007 to over three-quarters of a million. All this frenetic activity, however, wasn't to everyone's liking. One of the reasons why Facebook had became so devilishly infectious was that millions of office-bound young adults took to spending swathes of their working day inconspicuously staring out of virtual windows on their computers onto social networking sites. Particularly among young adults who were new to the world of work, hanging out online had soaked up much of what we used to think of as workplace gossip, those tall stories you might tell about the weekend, those half-hearted attempts at flirtation that help pass the working day. Prominent London companies got together to announce a crackdown on the use of Facebook, but to little avail. A survey published in the summer of 2007 claimed to have discovered that 233 million hours were lost every month as a result of British employees 'wasting time' on social networking sites. In a single day, on the eve of the British football season in August, more than 120,000 office hours had been squandered as fans put the finishing touches to their online fantasy football teams. In the same month, the Facebook network 'I have dossed around on Facebook all day and consequently have done no work' swelled to 240 members.

Whinges about employee productivity were not the only reason for frustration with sites such as Facebook. With this new kind of traffic coursing through the internet, many office-workers were puzzled to discover that their connections to the internet had ground to a halt. In just a few years, internet traffic moving directly between peers had grown to exceed the amount of one-way traffic going straight to sites on the web. This kind of peer-to-peer traffic had started as a way of sharing music files, but the same principle was soon being borrowed for sharing films and video clips, using webcams and playing online multi-player games. By 2006, three-fifths of all traffic coursing through the internet was made up of peer-to-peer connections forged under the radar of the world wide web. Then there were social networking sites like Facebook and DIY video broadcasters like YouTube which routed their traffic through a website, but only so as to enable communication between peers. By the middle of 2007 such was the pressure on the system that many began to fear that the internet, a patchwork of small and local networks, might not be able to take the strain. It was, according to some Cassandras, going to end in a monumental traffic jam.

In the gloomy years in which financiers closed the door on it, the strangest thing had happened: life on the internet began to enjoy a second coming. In the course of just a few years, as broadband connections became widespread and opened up a permanent window onto the web, many of us zoned out at work or disappeared off to the spare room to spend hours watching and communicating with each other online. No longer content with gawping at flashy websites on the internet, we began to build our own castles on its turf.

This surge in traffic travelling between ordinary users of the internet was, in some ways, quite predictable. Throughout the nineties the only way to connect to the internet was via a screechy dial-up modem. When people did manage to get through they wanted little more than to be able to check their e-mail and get out as soon as they could. After the technology bubble burst in March 2000 all those high-tech fibre-optic cables designed to provide super-fast broadband connections were left in the ground. Then, slowly, demand began to catch up with supply, and in an unprecedented way. Beginning at the turn of the millennium, the internet's second wind took its cue from the rise of a matrix of sites populated not by professionals but by millions of ordinary users. The first sign of things to come, as we saw in Chapter 2, was the birth of decentralised, lawyer-dodging systems for file-sharing that flourished after the fall of Napster, sites that were much more difficult to close down because there was no central administrator to sue. To their enthusiasts, these new sites were called 'peer-to-peer' communication; the term quickly grew to encompass just about any kind of communication among ordinary people via the internet. Then there was the rise of the people-powered internet search engine Google, the online auction site eBay and the proliferation of online diaries by bloggers. The first encounter that most people had with an online social network came courtesy of school reunion sites like Friends Reunited in the UK and Classmates.com in America. Friends Reunited was launched in July 2000 by Stephen and Julie Pankhurst, a husband-and-wife team from London who wanted to satisfy their curiosity about what their old friends from school were up to; in a single year its membership catapulted from three thousand to 2.5 million.

After the success of this first tranche of social networking sites came the launch of glossier, calling-card emporia aimed at young people. Friendster arrived in 2002 and a year later was followed by MySpace, which found a huge audience among teenage music-lovers. The arrival of Facebook on American campuses in 2004 was an opportunity for a posher and slightly older crowd to catch up. In January 2005 another British-based husband-and-wife team rolled out Bebo. Bebo was also designed to appeal to an older crowd but, to the utter surprise of its founders Michael and Xochi Birch, it was immediately adopted by millions of teenagers in Britain, Ireland, North America, Canada, New Zealand and Australia as their social networking site of choice. As the technology improved, along came video sharing. YouTube was rolled out in 2005, and quickly grew to account for 10 per cent of the bandwidth on the entire internet. The following year came Twitter, a pared-down version of Facebook's status updates that allowed its users to send their friends a running commentary of 'tweets' about what they were up to. The social networking land-grab was not limited to English-speaking countries. While Facebook and MySpace set the pace in North America and Europe, Orkut and hi5 spread like a Mexican wave through the countries of Central and Latin America, and Friendster, which had once ruled the roost in North America, went on to become the biggest social networking site in the Asia-Pacific region. Then there were those locally produced sites that often passed Western observers by: CyWorld, for example, has been up and running in South Korea since 1999 and now has nearly half of the South Korean population on its books. In an entirely spontaneous flight, which occurred over the space of just a few years, masses of ordinary people around the world quietly migrated to a vast electronic terrain where they could rub along with their online peers. Hitched to a continuous online information loop for long periods of time, they moved to Cyburbia.

For anyone with a long memory this mass migration was not an entirely fresh development. In many ways it mirrored the flight of an earlier generation of non-conformists, hippies who had fled San Francisco in the late sixties to set up a new, more egalitarian series of communes beyond the reach of mainstream society. Whereas the notion of the information highway in the late nineties had been a one-way suggestion for how to improve the flow of information from the mass media into our homes, this new kind of migration was more akin to a social movement. Just like the hippies before them, those who signed up to social networking sites did so because they wanted to spend time in direct and authentic communication with their peers. This time they had on their side not alternative ideas about politics and culture but an alternative idea about how to use new technology. Its promise was nothing less than to level hierarchies of all kinds, and to do so by tying people together with greater efficiency than had ever been accomplished before. The idea that this exchange of information between peers on an online network was about to change everything before it began to gain ground. It would do so by establishing a continuous online information loop to put millions of ordinary people back in touch with each other as online peers, thus merrily short-circuiting the need for any kind of authority, government or control, and stretching everything to be perfectly flat and leaderless – and leaving bureaucracies and hierarchies, without any means of controlling information, to collapse.

The hippies were not the only architects of this brave new world of peer-to-peer communication. Long before they came along, Norbert Wiener had pioneered the study of messages as a way of controlling both machines and society, and had

predicted the arrival of a non-hierarchical society governed by
a continuous stream of those messages. It was Wiener, remember, who had looked forward to a society knitted together by
highly responsive human messengers, each firing off messages
and instantaneously adjusting themselves to feedback on a
never-ending information loop. Even before the appearance of
online social networking sites there were portents that something similar was in the offing. Our enthusiasm for staring at
each other via CCTV cameras and broadcast television was a
good indication that we were ready to play a more active role
in communication networks. As we shall see in the next chapter, the fact that many of us had grown up playing computer
and video games, nimbly pressing buttons and adjusting ourselves to a constant stream of information to control the game,
was another clue that we were ready for life in a world defined
by rapid response to electronic feedback. Then there was the
explosion of text messaging and e-mail in the late nineties –
further evidence of an insatiable appetite for chatter with an
extended network. Those cybernetic information loops, however, were only played out within an extended circle of friends
and were merely electronic potty training for what lay ahead.
Only when digital throngs spontaneously arrived to crack open
that information loop and add themselves as nodes on online
social networks was Wiener's cybernetic vision fully realised.
As armies of human nodes queued up to send and receive a
constant stream of messages from their electronic ties, they
unknowingly become the infrastructure and the backbone of a
new kind of network or continuous information loop.
Information still had to be sent over a computer network
rooted in technology and wire cables, but the most important
kind of network on the people's web was no longer technology

or sockets but us, huddled in anonymous groups and busily
ferrying messages to and fro.

There was something unnervingly new here, too, for anyone
who cared to look. As millions volunteered to upload the
minutiae of their lives to digital networks and to spend vast
tracts of their time there, the clumsy network metaphor that
had been talked up over so many years as a way of explaining
how humans behave began to look much more sensible,
because no longer was it just an image. Now we really were
human nodes or sockets on an electronic network, and at least
for the time that we spent there we would find ourselves treating each other as such. Just ten days after his twenty-third
birthday, on 24 May 2007, Mark Zuckerberg shuffled on stage
in a San Francisco warehouse to explain the secret of Facebook's
triumphant success to journalists and computer developers.
Dressed in the traditional uniform of the computer geek –
Adidas sandals, jeans and a fleece – Zuckerberg looked even
younger than his years and seemed nervous, speaking in fal-
tering gulps as he struggled to read the screen that was
presumably feeding him his lines. Despite this, his audience
had been won over even before he said anything. 'Today,
together,' Zuckerberg announced to a rush of applause, 'we're
going to start a movement.' Projected onto the wall behind
him was a diagram that, at least to the uninitiated, looked like
a map of the world's airports and the myriad lines of connection between them. It wasn't airports that Zuckerberg wanted
to connect but people. In the same way that cartographers had
toiled for centuries to chart an accurate map of the world,
Zuckerberg saw himself as an explorer of the virgin terrain of
Cyburbia – one whose quest was to chart or map a 'social
graph' of the real and pre-existing ties and relationships of

which our lives are made up. By building a digital replica of who knows whom among those different ties and connections, Zuckerberg told his audience, he could make communication among them easier and more efficient. More than that, his social graph could lock them together in a network – 'a series of nodes and connections', as he put it, 'with the nodes individuals and the connections the friendships'. In portraying Facebook as a network made out of human nodes and the many different connections that arise to tie them together, Mark Zuckerberg was trying to make a link between the power of online social networks and older communications systems like the telephone or the fax machine. In short, he argued that Facebook had given our online communication network effects.

Zuckerberg's insight was that people get their information from the media on the one hand and from family and friends on the other. The former had already transferred most of its wares into digital technology; what he was trying to do was to amplify the latter by rendering it in digital form too. In doing so, he believed he could open people's eyes to the very many ties that secretly bind them to each other without anyone ever knowing. People would need to investigate the hidden web of social connections by themselves, of course, but their natural curiosity about who knew whom in their extended circle would spur them to do that. Zuckerberg was Facebook's cartographer-in-chief, but what he was offering us was the chance to become map-makers of the universe of our weak electronic ties that had always existed but had only now become visible in Cyburbia. The only way to navigate the contents of Facebook, after all, is through serendipitous hopping from the profile of one of your friends to one of their friends and so on.

As a result, the old saw that you know a person by the company they keep applies doubly on Facebook; the paucity of people's profiles there mean that just about the only way of knowing someone is via the company they keep there. Just as the network theorists had long insisted, in Cyburbia it was going to be at least as important to map the relationships between people as to know anything about those people themselves.

That wasn't the only way in which the principles of social network theory had acquired a new credibility. Set up to pass information speedily from one place to another, it is hardly surprising that the internet turned out to be a very potent way of ferrying our information around. As people learned how to pass on information and messages to their peers via e-mail, instant messenger and then online social networking sites, communiqués began to whizz around the world at breakneck speed on a giant global information loop. Very few of us had been in the habit of phoning up numbers from the telephone book at random to impart information, for example, but now we were more than happy to pass it on to our network of weak electronic ties. As we spent more of our time sending and receiving messages on this giant information loop, the speed with which traffic was able to zip around Cyburbia began to make the formerly outlandish hypotheses of social network theorists – those who argued that society could be analysed in terms of a computer network – look strangely perspicacious. As we saw in the last chapter, social network theorists had for many years been arguing that weak ties between people who didn't necessarily live in the same place could be amazingly powerful at ferrying parcels of information from one place to another, and infinitely speedier than relying on communication between friends. At least with regard to the time that we spent in the information routes of Cyburbia, that theory now looked to have come true.

Since this information flew around without being filtered through real discussion it also tended to be less credible. In keeping with the underground ethos of the internet and its instinctive mistrust of central authority, the traffic racing around Cyburbia tended to offer a more informal, gossipy and intimate gloss on events than anything offered by authority or by the mainstream media. While groups of people with strong ties to one another might have thought through the meaning of messages and their veracity before passing them on, now their cybernetic urge to rapidly forward them to their neighbours was given free rein. The power of the internet could be used to scotch rumours, and whisperings begun there made for an ideal way of rooting out falsehoods and bad faith among the authorities. Just as often, however, information passed from peer to peer could have perverse or even catastrophic results. As anyone who has ever batted back an e-mail without thinking knows, the almost instantaneous cycle of messaging and feedback that characterises life in Cyburbia seems to leave little time to reflect upon information before passing it on. Held aloft by peers on an electrical information loop and passed around as soon as it became available, information became contagious as a virus, flying from peer to peer in the blink of a cursor. Take an example. In 1996, the following message appeared in e-mail inboxes:

Did you see the recent Oprah Winfrey Show on which Tommy Hilfiger was a guest? Oprah asked Hilfiger if his alleged statements about people of color were true –

he's been accused of saying things such as 'If I had
known that African-Americans, Hispanics and Asians
would buy my clothes, I would not have made them so
nice,' and 'I wish those people would not buy my
clothes – they were made for upper-class whites.' What
did he say when Oprah asked him if he said these
things? He said 'Yes.' Oprah immediately asked
Hilfiger to leave her show. Now, let's give Hilfiger what
he's asked for – let's not buy his clothes. Boycott!
Please – pass this message along.

Millions of people did take the trouble to pass the message on,
despite the fact that Tommy Hilfiger hadn't made any such
statement and had never even appeared on Oprah's show. The
rumour refused to die even when Winfrey took the trouble to
deny it on TV. Even now it is still alive on some internet bulletin boards, and probably still being forwarded on.

Sending messages back and forth wasn't the only way to
occupy oneself in Cyburbia. For many of us, by far the best
thing about peer-to-peer communication was simply chatting with and hanging out with our friends. In 2007, while a
strike among Hollywood's scriptwriters hogged the headlines,
America's porn stars were struggling with an equally serious
threat to their own wilting careers. For as long as anyone
could remember, the porn industry could be relied upon to
make money, but by 2007 it was haemorrhaging talent and
laying performers off. The market for pornography in the
United States was worth thirteen billion dollars in 2005; two
years later its value had shrivelled to seven billion dollars. By
2008 the situation had gotten so bad that Larry Flynt, the

elder statesman of the US porn industry, predicted that half of America's porn producers would be out of business within the year. Porn companies, it could be argued, might have foreseen that their empire could go the same way as the music industry, with profits undermined by people's readiness to steal them away for nothing online. What they hadn't bargained for was the fact that their revenues would be depleted not only by peer-to-peer porn sites but from people simply talking to each other and checking each other out on the internet. By October 2006, looking for stuff using search engines such as Google had overtaken sex sites in popularity among British internet users. Similar statistics held for America. Between October 2005 and October 2007, according to the internet statistician Hitwise, visits to porn sites as a proportion of all American web traffic dropped by a third; among young Americans between eighteen and twenty-four, visiting porn sites had become less popular an internet pastime than chatting with other people using Facebook and MySpace, or perusing their online offerings using Google. Not only that, but closer investigation of the numbers revealed a curious correlation. In early 2008 a panel of American experts reported that the phenomenal rise of social networking operations 'almost perfectly' mirrored a downward turn in people ogling online pornography. When Facebook encountered problems with its server and become unusable for a few hours in 2007, there had been a correspondingly large spike in the numbers visiting porn sites. The only conclusion to be drawn was that people, and especially young people, were usually too busy ogling each other and sending messages to want to get off.

The porn business was only the most garish example of how established industry authorities had been undermined by the spread of peer-to-peer communication. Those involved in it, however, were in a worse pickle than even they imagined. Only a couple of years old, so-called 'porn sharing' sites with names like Pornotube, XTube and YouPorn were swallowing up the market for lascivious material. Just nine months after its launch in September 2006, YouPorn was adding fifteen million new viewers a month. Its website, according to some estimates, was doing more business than CNN. In December 2007, in a desperate attempt to protect its interests, Vivid Video, one of the world's biggest producers of adult films, filed a lawsuit against one upstart purveyor of online porn that invited viewers to upload clips so that other viewers could watch them for free. The problem was that its advisors had underestimated the nature and scale of the enemy it was facing. Vivid Video's lawsuit accused a DIY porn site of inviting its users to steal its copyrighted material and post it online for free, but everyone knew that the problem was more serious than that. It wasn't just pirated professional porn that was flooding peer-to-peer sites on the internet, but material that debuted millions of amateur porn stars. 'Some people say porn is porn is porn, but consumers have preferences,' one editor of an embattled porn industry magazine explained to a journalist. 'Some like amateur,' he conceded, 'with neighbours in their socks in a poorly-lit setting.' With a degree of professional pride, however, he noted that the vast majority of punters 'like a more polished product with high quality production and prettier girls doing fun things'.

By and large that simply wasn't true. The reason why people were going to peer-to-peer porn sites wasn't only because they wanted stuff for free. The teenagers who used peer-to-peer music sites didn't want to pay for their music, but they also wanted the rebellious thrill of routing around the control of the music industry. When that same principle arrived in the porn industry, it affected more than sales because it threw up a desire for something more grainily authentic than professional pornography could provide. A good many, as a consequence, had migrated to a vast virtual menagerie full of ordinary people exposing themselves either for their lover or everyone else to see. A survey of over 2500 Canadian undergraduates at the beginning of 2006 discovered that 87 per cent of them were conducting their sexual relationships by webcam, instant messenger or telephone. What many people wanted, it seemed, was nothing less than to be in a porn movie, or to watch other people appearing in movies of their own.

Ogling amateur pornography wasn't all we were doing with the time we spent staring out of our computer's window onto Cyburbia. In the internet equivalent of window-shopping, many of us found a new pastime in purposelessly drifting from one web link to another. In April 2007 a survey concluded that two-thirds of British internet users spent time 'wilfing' ('what was I looking for?') while browsing the internet. A quarter of those surveyed admitted to whiling away 30 per cent or more of their time on the internet in this way, the equivalent of spending one working day every fortnight lost in an electronic reverie. Daydreaming in Cyburbia could have real consequences. A third of the men surveyed admitted that wilfing has had a damaging effect on their relationships; the growing popularity of websites such as Friends Reunited is, in the opinion of the British marriage guidance body Relate, fuelling a hike in marital infidelity. In addition, under cover of the spare room many of us had become enthusiastic voyeurs, stalkers and curtain-twitchers. Take the phenomenon known as lifecasting, where people wire up a webcam to show a live feed of their entire domestic life. Lifecasting has its origins in 1996 when a twenty-year-old Pennsylvania student called Jennifer Ringley had the idea to sit a webcam in the corner of her college dorm and leave it on all the time. When she left college and moved into her own flat two years later, she added cameras to every room and began charging people for access to her website. Every day and night for seven years, what became known as JenniCam faithfully recorded every waking hour of Ringley's life as she doted on her many pets, sauntered around naked, slept, chatted with friends and generally went about her business. At one point JenniCam was receiving more than a million hits a day, one of which turned out to be Ringley's best friend who wasn't very pleased to discover that Ringley was sleeping with her fiancé. Ringley's experiment in lifecasting was soon being repeated by young people the world over, and before long someone made the discovery that, at least as far as the viewing audience was concerned, the life being cast did not even have to be human. JenniCam closed down in 2003, but in 2006 EagleCam started up when a Canadian called Doug Carrick began broadcasting images of a nest of bald eagles that had set up home in his backyard, and found an audience of ten million viewers a day. EagleCam had arrived on computer screens hot on the heels of the similarly themed PandaCam, and just before the momentous launch of Cheddarvision, where an audience of nearly a million people logged on to watch a lump of English Cheddar mature.

For many people this kind of viewing will sound crashingly dull, but to those who see it as a way to watch the world go by it must seem oddly intimate and reassuring. The cocktail of voyeurism and exhibitionism that makes staring out into

Cyburbia so popular an internet pastime surely owes a good deal of its audience to the thrill of circumventing the authority of the professional media and peering at something utterly unmediated. Borrowing from Norbert Wiener and Marshall McLuhan, the former hippie disciples of cybernetics who plotted how to put people back in direct communication with each other wanted to recreate the intimacy and authenticity of community life by building a new kind of electronic village. When their successors finally succeeded in levelling the terrain of the media to allow anyone into the loop, however, what they got looked more like a vast electronic suburb in which there was little else to do but spend vast amounts of time chattering and looking at ordinary people's lives.

In the summer of 2006 the most popular channel on the self-broadcasting internet site YouTube featured what appeared to be a sixteen-year-old girl called Bree sitting in front of a webcam and delivering a confessional-style account of her life in a series of mini-episodes. The first forty-six instalments of lonelygirl15, each no more than a few minutes long, became more intriguing as Bree's twee tales of her small-town upbringing gave way to darker hints about the mysterious religious rites practised by her parents. So charmingly tantalising was Bree's story and her delivery that lonelygirl15 quickly developed an avid following all over the world. Not everyone was happy, however. There was, in the opinion of many YouTube loyalists, something not quite right about lonelygirl15, and before long a posse of net aficionados had been rounded up to prove that she was not who she claimed to be. By the end of the summer they had succeeded. Lonelygirl15, it turned out, was not a lonely girl at all but a nineteen-year-old

actress and graduate of the New York Film Academy called
Jessica Rose; Rose, in turn, had been hired by a group of aspir-
ing filmmakers who thought posting something on YouTube
would be a good way to launch their careers. When word
spread that the people behind lonelygirl15 had been fibbing
all along, a groundswell of disgust rose up on the net. Masses
of bloggers and YouTube veterans descended, like armies of
Holden Caulfields, to label lonelygirl15 as nothing more than
a money-grubbing phony.

All this was a little unfair, because the makers of lonely-
girl15 were only doing their jobs. With sophisticated editing
and even a quirky soundtrack, the lonelygirl15 series of video
clips was of a much higher quality than most of what was on
YouTube, which was one of the reasons why so many of its
viewers kept coming back for more. In teasing YouTubers
about the authenticity of lonelygirl15, its makers were only
introducing a little dramatic playfulness into a genre long on
clips of cats dancing on pianos and short on stories that might
draw the viewer in. The brickbats hurled at lonelygirl15 were
also a little hypocritical, because communication on the internet was not quite as authentic as it was thought to be. Video
communication between peers certainly bypassed the spit and
polish of television producers and editors, but it was still communication funnelled through an electrical machine. Since the
cybernetic interface that hitched together humans and computers in a continuous information loop took the place of
face-to-face communication it was a medium just like any
other and, as Marshall McLuhan would surely have pointed
out, it was bound to have biases of its own. Lonelygirl15, for
example, kick-started the bandwagon of her success by
dropping into her conversations the names of several highly

influential YouTube users so as to attract the attention of their fans. What she was doing was called tagging – secreting key-words into her offering so that others on the YouTube network could seek her out. Tagging is very different from the tradi-tional forms of promotion or publicity found in the mainstream media, but is utterly essential to life on the inter-net because it helps people who spend time there to see and be seen. Since much of what we do on the internet involves using search engines, when people tag themselves or their texts, photos or keywords it helps us get where we want to go with the greatest efficiency. Think of tags as the shopfronts that illuminate the narrow streets of Cyburbia. In Cyburbia's lev-elled terrain there are almost as many shops as there are shoppers. As a result, unless your store is festooned with ban-ners stating who you are and what it is that you're selling, very few people will bother to go in.

Not everyone who posts their material on the internet wants everyone else to see it, but many of us do want to be noticed by our peers and tagging ourselves helps us to bring that about. Teenagers and young adults, who have been raised in Cyburbia, tend to be better at it. Two-thirds of Americans between the ages of twelve and seventeen who spend time online, according to a detailed study published in December 2007 by the Pew Internet Project, have cobbled together some kind of digital content and uploaded it directly to the internet in places like MySpace or Flickr; in doing so they learn very quickly to tag that content for names and themes that might interest passers-by. The combination of voyeurism and exhibitionism that seems endemic to life in Cyburbia is often blamed on young people's determination to let it all hang out, but maybe they are only moderating their behaviour to the nature of the medium; they need to show off who they are because otherwise they might never find an audience or find what they're looking for. Join a social networking site and you will immediately be invited to build an elaborate profile of yourself. Frequent visitors to these sites learn how to present themselves to best win the approval of their peers. A tag or profile need not necessarily be strictly accurate. Facebook residents who plaster their profiles with pictures of their better-looking friends, according to researchers at Michigan State University, are in turn more likely to be considered better looking by their peers than those who can only produce ugly friends. Likewise, those who design their own avatars in online games and social networking universes such as Second Life often take the opportunity to change their age, gender, race or class. One study of online gamers by British psychologists found that a majority had switched gender when filling in their profile at the beginning of the game. Women were more likely to undergo a virtual sex change than men – 70 per cent of female players told researchers that they usually preferred to be male avatars. In our television-saturated age, as the journalist-scholar Thomas de Zengotita has pointed out in *Mediated: How the Media Shape the World Around You*, many of us have unconsciously become very savvy media professionals, highly skilled when confronted by a camera because years of watching TV has taught us exactly how to behave. As we spend more time in Cyburbia, however, we are learning how to perform in whole new ways – this time not from professional broadcasters but from the experience of spending time stalking our peers and attempting to impress them. Some of us, a little like lonelygirl15, are even practising with almost professional guile the art of being an amateur.

There is something else we are getting used to. Just as privacy wasn't highly valued in tribal societies, it is no use at all in Cyburbia. In the company of our electronic peers many of us are more than happy to share vital information about who we are or who we want people to think we are. Spending time there can also lead us to relax our inhibitions, to say things and behave in ways that they would never normally consider. Learning to trust one's electronic peers can also lull people into a false sense of security. Since the year 2000 Tremor, a marketing campaign devised by the consumer goods giant Procter and Gamble, has been using the internet to enlist a panel of nearly 230,000 American teenagers (roughly 1 per cent of all American teens) who, in return for gifts, are supposed to promote its toiletry and perfume brands in internet chatrooms; in October 2005 the firm was reported to the American Federal Trade Commission by an advertising watchdog for failing to have its panellists disclose that they had been enlisted to help sell products. In its response, the FTC admitted that: 'In some word-of-mouth marketing contexts it would appear that consumers may reasonably give more weight to statements that sponsored consumers make about their opinions or experience with a product based on their assumed independence from the marketer.'

Not only can electronic peers not always be sure who they're talking to, but the anonymity and equality that attracted them to Cyburbia often turn out to be illusory. Since everything written in electronic ink usually leaves a clue as to its origins, it is not very difficult to work out who anyone is and use their information against them. At the same time that electronic tagging was being floated as a highly controversial way of coping with rising prison populations and the profiling of everyone from customers to potential terrorists was treated with grave suspicion, it is striking that so many of us are happily profiling and electronically tagging ourselves in Cyburbia for the benefit of our online peers. That this information could subsequently be used against us by the authorities or by employers barely registered, because we were convinced we had given them the slip.

When pieces of information on the net are tagged for relevance, the speed at which peers with similar interests can discover one another can be nothing short of breathtaking. In the autumn of 2007 I was summoned to interview Thomas Enraght-Moony, the fresh-faced and freshly installed CEO of the world's largest online dating service, Match.com, which claims twenty million members around the world. Just like many other industries, for some years Match.com had been under pressure from peer-to-peer operations like Facebook that allowed like-minded people to meet without the help of a paid chaperone, and Enraght-Moony was preparing to go on the offensive. When I asked whether the efficiency with which people can tag or profile themselves on Match and Facebook, and zoom in on those who meet their requirements might not be a little too quick, his response was to tell me a story. A good friend of his, he told me, walked every day to and from a train station in New England only moments away from the woman who would subsequently become his wife. While he turned left to exit the station to go home from work, she turned right. Living only a few miles apart they would never have met and fallen in love had it not been for the internet and Match.com.

Enraght-Moony's paean to the internet's ability to bring like-minded people together sounded impressive, but what it left out were the problems that arise when people with apparently similar interests can discover one another so rapidly. Bringing people together solely on the basis on an electronic checklist is giving rise to a series of walled gardens in Cyburbia, where people only encounter those who share their own opinions or interests rather than anyone who might challenge them. Sometimes the internet's facility for putting together people with similarly blinkered beliefs can be downright unnerving. In only a few years there has grown up a movement of over two hundred pro-anorexia ('pro-ana') websites in which young women get together to give each other tips on how not to eat and how to lose even more weight – one contributor advises drinking ice-cold water on the basis that 'your body has to burn calories to keep your temperature up'. Disturbed teenage boys can goad and influence each other in much the same way. In November 2007 a Finnish teenager called Pekka-Eric Auvinen strolled to school carrying a gun and proceeded to shoot dead eight students and teachers before turning the gun on himself. Before he did so, he posted a rant about the fakery and lack of authenticity of television and of those who watch it on YouTube, and paid tribute to a roll-call of schoolboy killers such as those who had shot up Columbine High School in Colorado in 1999. The police raided his computer and it seemed highly probable that he had been in electronic conversation with a fourteen-year-old from Philadelphia called Dillon Cossey, who had been apprehended the previous month while planning a shooting spree of his own. When another Finnish student, twenty-two-year-old Matti Juhani Saari, shot dead ten people and then himself in a school in September 2008, the officer leading the investigation claimed that it was 'very likely' he had been in touch with Auvinen. Both had been members of a small group, formed around a Finnish social networking site and YouTube, which was bound together by a shared fascination with school shootings. Just like Auvinen, too, Saari had posted a threatening video on YouTube before going on his shooting spree.

Those instances in which disturbed people seek out and find people exactly like themselves are only the most extreme manifestation of peer influence in Cyburbia. The point of peer-to-peer communication, remember, was to put an end to the power of gatekeepers and authorities to control what we should watch, read or listen to and put us back into direct communication with a community of our equals. As soon as we arrived there, however, it turned out that we needed the assistance of our fellow inhabitants to help us sort through the clutter. Think about what Google does. Like most search engines, it works by crawling the web, taking regular digital snapshots of what's out there, indexing it and rendering it accessible to anyone in search of anything. That still leaves its engineers the job of ranking the information that Google has made it its business to serve up. Though the company protects its ranking technology as assiduously as Coca Cola protects the recipe for its distinctive sugary drink, Google's most essential ingredient is known to be its PageRank algorithm. PageRank was the brainchild of Google's founders, Larry Page and Sergey Brin, who met while both were graduate students at Stanford University. Inspired by the academic tradition in which good scholarly articles are cited by one's peers and that list of citations used as a measure of influence and standing in the academy, the pair thought that they could apply much the same principle to work out how the information they were indexing should be ranked and displayed to the user. A clever indicator of a web page's relevance could be had not via any objective ranking of its value but by counting up how many people were pointing at it from their own websites and then measuring the weight and worth of all those pointing links by tracing how many people were pointing to them in turn – weighing up, in other words, the worth of a piece of information by drawing a detailed map of how many and what kinds of other people found it worthwhile. Long before Facebook set itself up as a cartographer of the universe of weak electronic ties, Google had established itself as a map-maker of the myriad relationships between all those billions of pieces of information which exist out there on the web. But that wasn't all. As Google's search technology became more sophisticated it enabled its users to feed back into Google's information loop their own opinion of the information that Google sent their way. Every time we choose from the list of hits that Google serves us up in response to our search we are helping Google rank the information of our peers, and that information is in turn used to track the best destinations on the web. When Google decided to measure the worth of a piece of information by looking at how many other people found it worthwhile, it sewed into its operation a kind of feedback loop that helped traffic flow around Cyburbia much more quickly and smoothly. As a result, it became one of the richest companies on earth.

The kind of electronic feedback loop that fuels Google's searches works wonders, but it is far from perfect. Google's PageRank system, and others that followed in its wake, as Tim Berners-Lee explained to me, are becoming increasingly skewed by search engine optimisation firms who buy up links from an open market in order to route traffic in the direction of their clients. A more fundamental problem than commercial chicanery, however, is that the instantaneous cycle of instruction and feedback on an electronic information loop can introduce distortions all of its own. For example, eBay is stitched together largely by information feedback loops in which buyers and sellers are encouraged to rank each other's honesty and reliability. In an intriguing public statement in February 2008 the company announced that it was overhauling its feedback system, and would ban sellers from leaving negative comments about buyers. What was happening, eBay admitted, was that when buyers gave bad feedback to sellers they had bought from, those sellers were responding by leaving negative feedback of their own. Fear of incurring such retaliation had driven both buyers and sellers to award each other excellent but quite unwarranted feedback, and the system was in danger of collapsing into mutual back-scratching. eBay's feedback loop oiled the wheels of its online auction very nicely, but only by sparking a kind of electronic peer pressure whereby the first person to arrive at a decision in any exchange would likely find it echoed by those they were dealing with. The system resembled a kind of robotic dance routine in which one dancer's decision to step in one direction leads to everyone else automatically following suit.

The mutual back-slapping that characterises peer influence in Cyburbia helps us understand how just a few popular blogs have grown to lay claim to so much of the traffic there. One of the most arresting developments in the last few years has been the arrival of blogs written by ordinary people who have learned the habit of instantaneously publishing material on the internet. The blooming of millions of blogs is often considered a blow against the entrenched interests of elites, but things are not quite as simple as they look. The first bloggers to set up shop certainly found themselves in a level playing field, with each competing equally for the eyeballs of online readers. They were hugely dependent on attracting the attention of their peers in the blogosphere. Blogs don't usually advertise their wares, after all, and depend greatly for their traffic on attracting links from other weblogs that point readers in their direction. Since Google ranks its searches in a similar way, the effect is redoubled when people go there to search for information.

With such a system in place, it wasn't long before this Eden of peer-to-peer equality began to mutate into something else. A glance at the geography of the blogosphere is enough to show that a very small number of veteran bloggers have the vast majority of the readership entirely to themselves. Suspecting that something was up, in 2002 a New York University academic called Clay Shirky took a look at a sample of 433 blogs and totted up the number of links that pointed towards each. What Shirky discovered was that the structure of the place was 'crazily, wildly imbalanced' with less than 12 per cent of the blogs hogging half of the links. The reason was simple. Imagine that a large group of people are asked to name their ten favourite blogs and post a link to each of them on their own blog. Martha, the first arrival, will diligently search through as many blogs as possible and then put up a list of her ten favourites on her own site. The second arrival, Mike, could do much the same but he has a better idea. Chary of the work involved in sifting through millions of blogs in search of something worth reading, he can't help noticing the list of his predecessor and cherry-picking some of Martha's choices. Since the easiest way to navigate a path through the blogosphere is to rely on direction from our online peers, each new arrival after Martha and Mike will end up making their choices so as to reinforce the choices made by their predecessors. On top of the mutual back-scratching of bloggers who make it their business to link to each other's work, there quickly arose an information feedback loop that drove new traffic around in circles so as to favour those who got there first. There may well be very many millions of bloggers out there, but most of them are toiling away in the shadows because – no matter how much they tag or otherwise draw attention to themselves – no one is paying them any attention at all. The cake has already been cut, and only a very few veterans, most of them technology enthusiasts who pitched up on the internet long ago, have managed to get a piece.

It would, in some ways, be a mistake to make too much of this lack of equality among peers in Cyburbia. There is no way of getting around the need to make decisions about what is worth looking at; our time is limited and, especially when confronted with the abundance of material on the web, we are usually spoilt for choice. Traditionally we relied upon cultural commissars, commissioners, editors and other tastemakers to do all this sifting for us. New bands or songwriters, for example, were plucked from obscurity by radio DJs or record industry talent scouts and then hyped up with so much advance publicity that they could hardly fail to succeed. Their choices were not always perfect; some were tone-deaf, others downright corrupt. When an electronic feedback loop in Cyburbia is called upon to make decisions about quality however, it is surely significant that the decisions that this new medium arrives at are often deeply conservative or highly unpredictable – and sometimes both. In an intriguing experiment conducted in the last three months of 2004 and the first three of 2005, three social network theorists at Columbia University used the internet to invite over fourteen thousand young people to rate songs by relatively unknown bands and download the ones they liked. The researchers began by dividing their subjects into two groups. The first group they asked to make their decisions independently of each other while the second they allowed to see a rolling chart of how many times, in descending order, each song had been downloaded by others – telling them, in effect, which songs were most popular. When they came in, the results were clear. Those who could see the download charts tended to give higher ratings to the songs at the top of the chart and were more likely to download those songs. In other words, people tended to like songs more if other people liked them. This made the choices of those in the second group highly unpredictable, with a great deal depending on who rolled up to make their choices first. Identical songs were judged to be hits or flops depending on whether other people had been seen to download them earlier.

There is nothing new about facing pressure from our peers when it comes to making decisions about whether music is good or not. People have always been affected by the taste of those around them, and that susceptibility to influence helps them make up their own minds. The effect discovered by the Columbia University researchers, however, was much bolder and more specific than that. Just like Clay Shirky, what they discovered was an effect which throws everything out of kilter and amplifies the decisions of a few early arrivals into a random self-reinforcing spiral of continued popularity. Their findings suggested that, left to fend for ourselves in Cyburbia with only our online peers for direction, our decisions about quality and taste tend to get stuck in a self-perpetuating feedback loop. But here was the rub: as enthusiastic believers in social network theory, the researchers saw no problem in generalising data gleaned from a community of online peers to tell a story about how humans influence each other in everyday life. It didn't weigh very heavily upon them that the medium through which their study was conducted – an interactive website – might have prejudiced their results, and that the peer pressure they were talking about was specific to the way that information flows through an electronic loop whose operation is closed to the outside world. When they first envisaged cybernetic man, Norbert Wiener and the electro-hippies who had borrowed his ideas had imagined someone who existed on a continuous information loop, constantly firing off messages and adjusting himself to feedback about his environment and his effect on that environment. Now that our information loop had opened up to include everyone else with access to the internet, we couldn't help but adjust ourselves to an electronic loop of feedback about other people's choices just as soon as they were made. Confronted with a chart offering rolling feedback on other people's selections, what the Columbia University researchers had really discovered was that the inhabitants of Cyburbia would plump for what was already popular among their online peers, and that songs which managed a high initial chart position would find their position continually reinforced.

Our new home in Cyburbia was a stranger place than those early cybernetic believers could ever have imagined. New arrivals had been promised a world of equality, but as soon as they got there they discovered that some were a good deal more equal than others and that the pecking order had been decided long ago. Then there was the claustrophobia induced by living in constant communication with our neighbours. As more and more people piled in to Cyburbia to make their fortune, the sign-posts there became wilfully confusing. Despite the huge amount of traffic coursing through Cyburbia, much of it seemed to be going around in circles; despite the abundance of its population there was a marked tendency for people to hang out with people just like them and to conform to the opinion of their peers. Conversation in Cyburbia quickly degenerated into tittle-tattle. The popularity contests regularly held there were strangely combustible affairs, and had all the feel of being rigged.

Not that we really cared. Having grown up hitched to computers, video games and mobile phones, many of us were getting quite used to living our lives on a electronic information loop and rapidly responding to feedback from our peers. We were slowly getting the feel for our cybernetic body armour, and now we were going to use it to help us move around in the rest of our lives.

6

Non-Linear

In April 2002 several thousand Israeli soldiers massed on the
outskirts of the ancient West Bank city of Nablus. The subsequent Israeli assault on the city formed part of Operation
Defensive Shield, Israel's largest military intervention in the
West Bank since the 1967 war, and the Israeli Defense Forces
(IDF) justified their actions by claiming that gunmen from a
bewildering array of different Palestinian factions had con-
gregated on the city and made it their headquarters. Thus far,
there was nothing very unusual about the game of cat and
mouse played out between Israeli troops and Palestinian
gunmen. But then the Israelis were seen to be moving
through the city in a highly unusual manner. Instead of using
the streets, alleys, courtyards and doors which criss-crossed
Nablus and defined its geography, reports soon emerged that
the Israeli soldiers had been punching holes through the
walls, ceilings and floors of Nablus's buildings with
explosives and huge hammers, thereby forging their own

distinctive route through the city. Most of the intense fighting that followed took place in living rooms, bedrooms and corridors, with soldiers sometimes throwing stun grenades to shock frightened occupants into submission. When the battle subsided and the dust settled the Israelis had not only beaten back the Palestinian fighters. They had changed the geography of the city and established new pathways through Nablus.

This novel military manoeuvre pioneered by the IDF during Operation Defensive Shield became known as 'walking through walls'. It was not done on a whim, but was the product of many years of deliberation at the heart of the IDF. In the years before their assault on Nablus, it emerged, the Israelis had set up several think tanks dedicated to understanding how to deal with the low-intensity urban warfare they were now engaged in against Palestinian factions in the Occupied Territories. The most influential of those think tanks was known as the Operational Theory Research Institute (OTRI). With an enemy splintered into many different armed groups sponsored either by Fatah, Hamas or Islamic Jihad, and each of those groups conducting their own manoeuvres in the city, the thinkers at the OTRI argued that regular armies needed some new tricks in their armoury. Given the unpredictability of the terrain and the many-headed nature of the enemy, they suggested that there would be little point in relying exclusively upon an ordered and regimented battle plan handed down from command headquarters. What was required was a new kind of agility among soldiers so that they could rapidly respond to a constant stream of new information about their environment, and new kinds of tactical manoeuvre to help those soldiers move around.

One of the buzzwords associated with this new kind of militarism was that soldiers should learn how to be non-linear in their movements. What it meant was that, in addition to following a hierarchical chain of command, units would henceforth be encouraged to communicate with each other via new technology and constantly adapt their movements to events on the ground; instead of following a chronological plan of action they would be encouraged to use their own initiative as they encountered new information. When an architect subsequently tried to make sense of the incursion into Nablus by excavating the routes taken by the Israeli soldiers, it was discovered that over half of the buildings in the centre of the city had routes forced through them, with each of those buildings pock-marked with between one and eight openings. These newly bull-dozed routes through Nablus could not be described as linear and orderly pathways. They were chaotic and without clear direction, allowing for many different points of entry and exit. The path taken by the soldiers of the IDF was a delib-erate zigzag – it was non-linear not only in the sense that it followed no particular order, but also in the sense that it had been made up as the soldiers took delivery of new electronic information about the position of their enemies. At the time of the incursion it was described by the com-mander in immediate charge of the operation, Aviv Kochavi, as a 'reorganisation of the urban syntax by means of a series of micro-tactical actions'. In other words, instead of submit-ting to the established pathways offered by the layout of Nablus the soldiers had cut up that geography and reassem-bled it to suit their own purposes. Overnight the architecture of an ancient and impermeable city was transformed into something with all the fluidity and freedom for manoeuvre of a computer game.

The story of our growing attachment to life on an electronic information loop has reached our arrival in a place called Cyburbia. Thus far, we have only discussed the most visible manifestation of Cyburbia: our migration to online social networks in order to spend time ceaselessly passing information back and forth between ourselves. Cyburbia, however, has been a long time in the making and its influence goes far beyond the time that we spend on the internet. As we shall see in the following chapters, it has already spread out to affect our sense of direction, how we think and our ability to pay attention, how we engage with culture, the media and our institutions, even how we go to war.

Let's start with our sense of direction. That the Israeli Army turned to cybernetics to help them reinvent the art of combat at the beginning of the twenty-first century was not entirely surprising. The discipline, as we have already seen, had its origins in research carried out by an inter-disciplinary group of mathematicians and scientists to help the Allies win the Second World War. Like most new inventions, it arose as the answer to a very practical problem. In 1940 the British anti-aircraft gunners whose job it was to shoot down Luftwaffe bombers found that their efforts were almost worthless. Their job was complicated by the efforts of the bomber pilots themselves, whose constant and deliberately evasive zigzagging made it almost impossible for British anti-aircraft gunners to get a reliable bead on their position and shoot them down. It was difficult enough to try to predict and compute the flight path of an aeroplane when it was flying in a straight line; what the anti-aircraft gunners needed was a way of factoring into their equations the constant zigzagging operation of the pilots who were trying to shake them off. The result was not only a technological fix, but a whole new philosophy of man and his relationship to electrical machines. Cybernetics predicted the birth of a new kind of man who, armed with communications technology like both the anti-aircraft gunner and the bomber pilot, had as his defining feature the ability to be rapidly responsive to a continuous stream of messages, and ever ready to adjust his movement to all this feedback. It was exactly this kind of cybernetic man that, sixty years later, the boffins of the Israeli Defense Forces wanted their soldiers to be.

What does it really mean to move in a non-linear way through electronic information, using a continuous stream of that information as our guide? A good way to imagine it is to return to the military origins of cybernetics and that battle of wits between anti-aircraft gunner and the bomber pilot. Just like the pilot of the German bomber or the British anti-aircraft gunner, the person navigating their way through electronic information is constantly moving around and adjusting her aim and her flight path in response to a continuous stream or loop of information. Like the enemy pilot, the result is to make her flight path look like a jarring and unpredictable zigzag. Navigating a path like this through electronic information, it turns out, is about much more than not moving in a straight line. It's about what Marshall McLuhan called 'a revulsion against imposed patterns', the systematic and stubborn refusal to take the road made available and a determination to choose your own path by keeping abreast of a continuous stream of information. Like the flight path of the bomber pilot and the aim of the anti-aircraft gunner, the path we take through electronic information can be reduced to two words – 'zigzag' and 'adjust'.

But just how did we learn it? When Tim Berners-Lee developed hypertext into the world wide web in 1990, as we saw in Chapter 4, he enabled us to amble airily around the internet, hopping from one place to another and tracing our own singular path through the information trail. Most of us have been using a computer mouse and the web for little more than a decade and yet we have taken to zigzagging around in response to electronic information as if it were second nature. At least part of the answer is that, long before e-mail and the internet, before anyone even imagined having any need for a mobile phone or a mouse, millions of young people around the world were quietly practising by sitting, usually in a trance-like state in the dark, in front of a computer game.

Think about what happens when a computer gamer sits like an electrified zombie in front of a screen and presses a button on a keyboard, twiddles a joystick or clicks a mouse. He does so in order to affect a change or movement on screen, and he proceeds to observe the movement that results on the screen immediately afterwards. Having observed the result of his actions the player uses that movement as feedback with which to evaluate his next movement or adjustment on screen. The whole sequence usually takes place so rapidly and repeatedly that it becomes a continuous loop or circuit; information is received and acted upon almost automatically, and as a result of that continuous loop of information the player very quickly learns how to make sudden choices and split-second decisions. Without thinking about it he becomes an expert in the art of rapid electronic response. That, however, is only to think about

the game's information loop from one end. As the player learns
to zigzag to outwit the baddies in a computer game, the game,
if it is sophisticated enough, is also learning to track his where-
abouts and is discreetly forwarding a continuous loop of
information about the direction in which he is headed to the
baddies who are chasing him. As the player learns to adjust his
aim to shoot more of the enemy, the game keeps track of
his adjustments and passes it to the baddies to help them out.
In the battle to the death between the player and the game, the
game becomes a cybernetic actor as much as the player. It
needs to do so if it is to keep the player engaged, and to stand
a chance of beating him.

I know all this because I was that electrified zombie. The
first computer game I played as a teenager had the ignomin-
ious title Jet Set Willy, and was produced in 1984 for a thin,
rubbery little computer called the Sinclair ZX Spectrum. The
plot was so simple as to be inane: a newly wealthy character
called Willy, illustrated by a threadbare and barely recognis-
able visual persona, was charged with tidying up all the items
left around his house after a huge party. His prize, if he got
that far (I never did) was to be allowed access to his master
bedroom by his housekeeper. The play area consisted of sixty
different rooms or screens and the novice gamer was confronted with layer upon layer of stairs, walkways and ropes
and invited to walk from left to right and avoid the monsters
looming along the way. With only three controls – left, right
and jump – and manoeuvrability guided by either the joystick or the computer keyboard, Jet Set Willy was never
going to feature on any checklist of aspirations that parents
had for their children. Among teenagers like myself who had
never seen a computer before and who only had films and

books for company, however, it was a revelation and an instant hit.

Jet Set Willy was just one in a series of computer and video games that arrived, like ET, in the bedrooms of teenagers around the world in the eighties, and subtly changed their outlook on the world. Others included such classics of misspent youth as PacMan, Donkey Kong and Super Mario Bros. All of them came with very simple back-stories, but those elementary attempts at plotting always took second place to the games' intense playability. In each case players were sent off on a trudge through a series of tasks or levels and teased with points, rewards and incentives as they went along. As the technology became more sophisticated, so too did the games. The first computer game I ever played as an adult came with the Apple Mac that I bought as a graduate student, and it was called Wolfenstein 3D. Wolf 3D was a ridiculously bad-taste affair, a take-no-prisoners raid on a Nazi-occupied castle by a heavily armed and trigger-happy soldier who was confronted at every turn by rabid attack dogs and pot-bellied Nazis straining to shout 'Achtung!' and fire their weapons at the same time. All the same, when it appeared it was generally considered to be a breakthrough, the first of a glut of 'first-person shooter' games that became enormously popular on home computers in the middle of the nineties. What was novel about these first-person shooter games was not only their better graphics, but that everything appeared in 3D and from the perspective of the player who was staring down the barrel of a gun. Castle Wolfenstein was a Gothic hellhole in three glorious dimensions, but that wasn't the only thing impressive about it. What made the game so playable was the greater space afforded to players to make their own way around the castle. The game still came with a simple and perfunctory back-story, and it was still played in a highly linear series of levels, each of which had to be completed before moving on to the next, but it also allowed its players greater choice and greater freedom of manoeuvre.

Why were Jet Set Willy and Wolfenstein 3D so playable, and what did playing them do to people like me? Those who spend long periods of time playing games, especially from an early age, tend to become highly skilled in hand-eye coordination and manual dexterity. A string of scientific studies has shown that adults who have spent even short periods of time playing computer and video games are better able to switch their attention between different tasks, and are more capable of responding to new information rapidly, than those who haven't. In 2002 a study by doctors at the Beth Israel Medical Center in New York found that young surgeons who had played video or computer games were significantly more likely to be skilled at the fine art of keyhole surgery than those who had not. The researchers were not merely content to quiz their subjects about whether they'd played computer games as teenagers. In the study's last phase the baffled young surgeons were seated in front of popular computer games like Super Monkey Ball 2 – a game in which the player/monkey is asked to pilot a spherical ball around a series of obstacle courses – and told to play it to the best of their ability. Repeated sessions with Super Monkey Ball 2, the researchers concluded, not only improved hand-eye co-ordination among the surgeons but also improved their reaction times and their spatial awareness. The experience of having played these kinds of games was a better indicator of skill at keyhole surgery even than the number of years spent training or the number of medical procedures carried out.

Too much flighty button-pressing on an electronic information loop, however, and the danger is that we forget how to stay still or stand back long enough to appreciate what we are looking at. This is particularly true of those whose brains are not yet fully formed. Park little children in front of video games in which they learn only how to press buttons and respond rapidly to feedback, Susan Greenfield, Oxford University's Professor of Synaptic Pharmacology, told me, and it's not very surprising when they end up fidgety, hyperactive and unable to concentrate. Greenfield suspects that this kind of relentless electronic activity among children can lead to a craving for constant stimulation, which in turn often ends up being diagnosed as Attention Deficit Disorder, or ADD, a psychological syndrome said to be characterised by an unusual sensitivity to interruption. It is worth noting that Ted Nelson, the maverick who first coined the term 'hypertext' to describe our ability to navigate our own path through electronic information in 1965, has suffered since childhood from what later become known as ADD.

Learning how to respond to electronic feedback, and better hand-eye co-ordination, however, weren't the only things we picked up by spending all those hours playing computer games. We were also learning to crave greater freedom of manoeuvre as we made our way through their digital landscapes. Looked at in retrospect, Jet Set Willy, Wolfenstein and even Super Monkey Ball 2 were relatively simple attempts to engage the attention of game-players. At best they allowed players a little freedom as they jumped from rope to rope or took pot shots at overweight Nazis, but they were still bound by the convention that players should progress through different levels if they were to win or complete the game. Walk through any large video and computer games retailer today and Jet Set Willy and Wolfenstein look as old-fashioned as black-and-white television. Today's games, available on games consoles such as Microsoft's Xbox, Nintendo's Wii and Sony's PlayStation 3, as well as on computers, promise players the opportunity to influence and shape their own story and choose their own path through the game. Computer gaming has been growing up along with its players; the average gamer is no longer the stereotypical dysfunctional male in his unkempt bedroom but is, according to figures produced by the US Entertainment Software Association, aged thirty-five and with twelve years of gaming already under his belt – or her belt, as gamers are now almost as likely to be female as male. To impress this sophisticated audience, new games are launched with all the fanfare formerly associated with blockbuster films. In May 2008 the newest iteration of the popular video game Grand Theft Auto made five hundred million dollars in its first week in the United States, beating Hollywood's top-selling film, the latest instalment of the *Pirates of the Caribbean* franchise, into a humiliating second place.

The complexity of the back-stories in computer games often puts mainstream films to shame. For example, a great deal of hype surrounded the launch of one blockbuster sci-fi role-playing game called Mass Effect in November 2007. Its premise was a breathtakingly complex riff on mankind's struggle to find its feet in a universe governed by an alliance of alien races in the year 2183. Like Wolfenstein, the game looked like a tra-ditional first-person shooter, but it also promised to embroil players in a delicately woven storyline that allowed them to converse with a cast of beautifully drawn aliens, investigate countless unexplored planets, blast their way through a bevy of dangerous missions and take a wide variety of different paths through the story. The game included more than twenty-two thousand lines of realistic spoken dialogue, which stretched to four hundred thousand words. 'With games like this lasting for weeks and weeks,' one early reviewer from the Associated Press speculated, 'why even bother with commercial-filled televised space dramas you can't control?' Mass Effect might have sold itself as a thrusting intergalactic space opera of amazingly realistic operations but, by the time it arrived, it, and games like it, were firmly on the back foot. With its sophisticated graphics, complicated back-story and acres of dialogue, the reviewer from the Associated Press was right to observe that Mass Effect looked much more like a film than a game. The game's manufacturers, however, sought to promote it as a non-linear gaming environment in which each player was free to take their own route through the story. Strictly speaking, it was neither. Mass Effect wasn't like a story because it allowed the viewer too much freedom within it. Neither was it entirely non-linear in its game-play: since it had a beginning, a middle and an end that the player was encouraged to work towards it could not claim to be entirely without authorial direction. In the crackle of internet chatter that followed its release, the main reason why Mass Effect fell short of expectations was that it promised a truly non-linear environment in which gamers could make it up as they went along but had failed to live up to this. The reason for that, in turn, was that in the years between Wolfenstein and Mass Effect gamers had stumbled across something truly non-linear and were reluctant to go back. What they had discovered were virtual landscapes that allowed them to play not only against the game itself but against millions of their peers online – and they had migrated to Cyburbia in their droves to play them. These 'alternate universes' and 'massively multiplayer online role-playing games' include Second Life, World of Warcraft and EverQuest. To their millions of subscribers, who routinely play them for hours and even days at a time, they make for an unusually immersive experience. True, these virtual worlds often seduce their players with quests, rewards and incentives as they make their way through the game, but since each player is now playing against millions of others via an online information loop it is no longer entirely clear where the story began and where it will all end.

Take the phenomenon known as Second Life. A more rarefied twist on the idea of online social networking, it is, according to its website, 'a 3-D virtual world entirely built and owned by its residents' and a 'vast digital continent, teeming with people, entertainment, experiences and opportunity'. New inhabitants are invited to create an avatar and then walk it around to chat – via a keyboard and speech bubbles – to other residents, to purchase virtual land and to travel anywhere they want to go. Since opening its doors in 2003 Second Life has grown with ever-increasing vigour. In the month I joined, October 2006, it claimed its millionth inhabitant. By the summer of 2008 its population had grown to fifteen million. With its bespoke economy of Linden dollars, and its keen sense of entrepreneurship, some have compared Second Life to a virtual version of the board game Monopoly, played with millions of strangers. With its opportunities for illicit sex, endless boutiques and long stretches of boredom, however, spending long periods of time there reminded me more of how people used to think of life in the suburbs – full of secrets and intrigue punctuated by fitful attempts among strangers to get to know one another. Never make the mistake of telling any Second Life aficionado that this is all a game. There is, they point out, no objective or goal. It is much more lifelike than that.

That is precisely the point. Computer gamers have migrated in their millions to virtual universes in Cyburbia because they have had enough of being pushed around the place and wanted more freedom of movement than a traditional game played against the computer could allow. The new online multiplayer games and virtual worlds that hooked up millions of strangers around the world were largely without direction, progress or over-arching purpose – and that's precisely what made them so appealing. The ready-made back-stories and dialogue in which computer and video games had long sought to cloak themselves were never much more than decorative, but now more than ever they looked redundant. No longer did one thing have to follow on from another because now online peers had taken control of the story, and with everyone playing and strategising against everyone else it was impossible to predict how things would turn out. The best way to retain the attention of players, the success of these virtual worlds suggested, was not the anticipation of seeing the next level in the game but of seeing how a real player would react to your next move, even if was as simple as walking up and saying hello. Playing games against a computer was slowly giving way to playing against millions of other people via a giant online information loop. Many gamers had learned how to be anti-aircraft gunners; what they now wanted were real-life enemy pilots.

Try as they might, computer or video games can never really be proper stories. With its lavish budget, Mass Effect could afford a highly sophisticated back-story, but as soon as the action began that story juddered to a halt. The ability to tell a story properly, after all, requires that the storyteller not be waylaid by the wanderings of the audience. That's why when games are made into films they often disappoint gamers and non-gamers alike: the non-gamers wanted greater fluidity and skill in the storytelling, while the gamers get twitchy because they can't bear not being in on the action. Isn't it possible, though, that the greater freedom afforded us by digital information is affecting the kind of stories that we want to listen to? Might our cybernetic urge to forge our own path through information, as Marshall McLuhan predicted, now be too restless to cope with the traditional one-thing-after-another plotlines of mainstream culture?

One fashionable response to the internet has been to build stories in which the reader can directly participate, via digital technology, in the telling of the story – by pressing a button and choosing from a range of endings, or even by suggesting their own ending. Some storytellers have been playing around with this, but to little avail. According to some of the more breathless advocates of 'hypertext fiction' or 'hyper-fiction', a new literary genre which allows readers to make choices over the direction of the story using their mouse or their keyboard, today's readers and authors no longer want to read books in the same front-to-back way that their parents did. Thus far, however, not a single work of 'hyper-fiction' has proved to be worth reading. Maybe the reason why this kind of storytelling has failed to get off the ground is that it has forgotten about the basic need for the storyteller to tell a story. Stories are everywhere, and the reason that they are so popular is that they offer us meaning and a way of making sense of the world and our place in it. For as long as we humans have existed, stories have entertained us and helped us hand down knowledge and lore from generation to generation; they are so fundamental to us that they must somehow be hard-wired into our brains.

But what if Marshall McLuhan was right and the wiring is subtly changing? For many years now, just as he prophesied, the habit of reading books has slowly been losing its grip on many of us. What McLuhan couldn't very well have foreseen was that many people, particularly young people, would swap thumbing through paper books for reading on a computer screen. In itself, that need not be a problem. There is, as McLuhan pointed out, nothing particularly natural about the act of reading or writing stories. Given that the internet is stuffed with text, and overwhelmingly navigated through words, spending time on it is more likely to be a boon than a hindrance to literacy. When researchers in Michigan gave children and teenagers computers on the condition that they were allowed to monitor their use of the internet, they discovered that the grades and reading scores of those young people actually rose with the time that they spent online. What the invention of the book did manage to do was to impose a certain kind of order over how readers made their way through the text within, and over time the wiring of our brains adjusted to this. In comparison to the computer gamer or the internet user, the reader of a book has long been seen as passive and utterly at the mercy of the storyteller. He or she, after all, has precious little power over how the story is told. On the other hand, it's the humble reader who chooses how to interpret the work. Even in the most straightforward of novels, it's up to the reader to reassemble the component parts of the story in their minds and then scan it for meaning. Also, the author's control over how we read is not absolute: tire of a book and one can always turn its pages to find the sexy or interesting bits, like fast-forwarding a film.

Those of us who have got used to reading on screen have a much more powerful way of taking the reins from an author or an authority. Armed with our computer mouse, what would have been a book appears to us as a stream of messages on a loop, a loop that usually encourages us to hop around nimbly from one place to another. A study of reading habits published by the British Library at the beginning of 2008 found that readers who use screens were not reading in the traditional sense. The researchers identified a new kind of reading called 'horizontal information-seeking' – a kind of skimming activity, where readers don't read from top to bottom, but bounce around using search technology or hyperlinks. The average time that someone spends with an e-book, the researchers found, was no more than four minutes. 'It almost seems,' they concluded, 'that they go online to avoid reading in the traditional sense.'

What kinds of stories do people like these want? Look carefully at mainstream television and cinema and a new kind of storytelling that deliberately engages our restless, cybernetic imagination already seems to exist. Like the game of strategy between the anti-aircraft gunner and the enemy pilot, they allow the audience to adjust and zigzag their way through the story, not by giving away some physical control of the narrative like a computer game, but by adjusting themselves to a sensibility which will be familiar to anyone who has spent a great deal of time on an electronic information loop. These new kinds of stories are not structured in the traditional way: they are oblique and elusive enough to allow for a wide variety of interpretations, and broad enough to allow the reader to follow their own path through the narrative. Investigate the themes which drive them and they seem eerily similar, and more than a little reminiscent of the language of cybernetics. For the most part, the plots of these new stories emphasise chance, coincidence and random connections. They don't have an obvious beginning, middle or end; if they are thrown forward at all it is by bad luck, freakish twists of fate and the inability of characters to take things into their own hands and make sense of their lives. Like all good stories, these new narratives are invested with morals and meaning, but more often than not their meaning is that meaning itself is difficult to decipher. What is special about this new kind of storytelling in cinema and television, is that it is becoming increasingly non-linear.

Let's call it cyber-realism. A cyber-realist story contains at least one of four different elements: the puzzle, the loop, multiplicity and the tie. Sometimes a film comes along that showcases all four, and in 2003 that film arrived in the form of *21 Grams*. *21 Grams* was a bleak film that nonetheless marked the arrival in Hollywood of the celebrated Mexican writer-director team of Guillermo Arriaga and Alejandro González Iñárritu. Its plot revolved around a tragic hit-and-run road accident that resulted in the death of a father and two small daughters. Naomi Watts played the grief-stricken mother, a recovering drug addict flailing emotionally in the aftermath of the accident; Benicio Del Toro an ex-convict turned evangelical Christian who was trying to get his life back together before his erratic truck-driving left Watts's family dead; Sean Penn was a maths professor who, with a deteriorating heart condition and less than a month to live, was in dire need of a transplant and who was fortunate enough to receive a heart from one of the victims of the accident. Thus far, *21 Grams* didn't seem very different from the usual Hollywood fare. There was, however, something novel about the way in which the story was written and filmed. Just as in *Amores Perros*, the previous film by Arriaga and Iñárritu, and their subsequent star-studded block-buster *Babel*, *21 Grams* was a story that dealt with the overlapping, strangely myriad connections between three char-acters with vastly different existences who – if their lives had not been intertwined in a random tragedy – would not other-wise have met. Then there was the filming itself. The film was shot in chronological order and subsequently edited into a non-linear arrangement of sections that flicker back and forth between events before, during and after the accident. Watching it was a deeply confusing experience, and deliberately so. *21 Grams* set out to chop itself up into digital bits so as to chal-lenge audiences and to keep them on the edge of their seat. The disparate pieces of the story fitted back together like a jigsaw, a puzzle whose real meaning only became clear when all the pieces were in place. The film didn't have an obvious structure. Like that enemy pilot upon whom Norbert Wiener based his cybernetics, it zigzagged back and forth as if to deliberately confuse its audience, forcing it to constantly adjust its antennae to bring the plot closer into focus.

Films such as *21 Grams* are now all the rage in cinema, and not only in the art-house. Hammering together as it does three completely different stories in a resolutely non-chronological order, Quentin Tarantino's 1994 film *Pulp Fiction* was an early example of cyber-realist storytelling. Explaining the thrill he gets from telling stories in cryptic, non-linear fashion, Tarantino has claimed than he finds it fun 'to watch an audience in some ways chase after a movie'. *Pulp Fiction* and *21 Grams* were aimed at different audiences in different parts of the world, but both in their own way aimed to zigzag around the truth and create an air of insoluble mystery. They were far from alone. In more or less artful ways, storytellers of all kinds have been queuing up to stoke our suspicion that secret codes and patterns might exist tantalisingly out of reach and to taunt us with possible solutions. Yet another example of a paranoid mystery puzzle that is becoming more and more common in film and cinema is *Lost*, one of the most expensive and most popular American television series ever made.

Lost, which first aired in 2004, follows the tribulations of a group of air-crash survivors on a mysterious desert island. Twenty-five episodes in, the viewer is witness to a conversation between John Locke, a bald-headed mystic, and Jack, the programme's nearest thing to a leading man. Locke, whose shifty demeanour and gibbering mysticism leads one to suspect that he knows more about their predicament than he is letting on, is berating Jack for his lack of faith: 'Do you think this is an accident? That we, a group of strangers, survived, many of us with just superficial injuries? You think we crashed on this place by coincidence, especially *this* place? We were brought here for a purpose, for a reason, all of us.' Some years and many series later, viewers are still in the dark about what that purpose might be. Locke is right that the island is no ordinary place – it features polar bears who wander around the tropical island, a fat guy called Hurley who thinks everything can be explained by numbers, and a formless invisible blob that comes along every few episodes to chase some of the more out-of-shape characters through the jungle. It is also a runaway television success story.

The series boasts a huge cast of characters and a breathtaking number of plotlines; it works by piling puzzle upon impenetrable puzzle while stubbornly refusing to solve most of them. In search of a little enlightenment, its diehard fans have flooded on to the internet for clues on how to crack its determinedly enigmatic plot. Dip your toe into the blogosphere and you will be swept away by a wave of riffs on the meaning of *Lost*; musings on the significance of the different shades of light used, the colours of black and white, even the clothes worn by the characters. Wags have suggested that the island might be a tropical purgatory; that the plight of the characters might be an allegory for the state of contemporary America; that they might have got themselves caught in a time warp; that they are unwitting island-mates in some reality TV show; and – that old chestnut – that it might all be a dream. One intriguing interpretation of the series is that everything within it is part of a giant computer game. The inventor of the web, Tim Berners-Lee, told me that he is struck by the eerie similarity between *Lost* and a well-known computer game called Myst: both have their characters explore an apparently deserted island and attempt to solve a series of highly cryptic puzzles. It can hardly be coincidental that the writers of *Lost* have used lots of tropes and devices taken from video games. The locked hatch found by the characters in one series, for example, resembles games like Jet Set Willy and Donkey Kong in which players often find locked doors, and the means of opening them are not discovered until later on in the game. The random appearance of polar bears on the island must have sent gamers reaching for their joysticks as it is quite common in computer and video games to find wholly unexpected, out-of-place animals darting across the screen to confuse their players.

The second nudge to the viewer that they are watching a piece of cyber-realist storytelling is the appearance of a narrative loop that suggests that the story, rather than moving forward, might be about to turn back on itself. Just as the gurus of cybernetics predicted that linear, one-after-another processes would soon be replaced by continuously looping circuits of information, storytellers have begun to use narrative loops as a neat way to flip the expected chronology of their stories. *21 Grams* chops the linear narrative into digital bits so as to challenge the audience and engage its attention. The end of the film reverts to the beginning, as if all its events have been playing on a giant loop and are fated to be replayed again and again. A common way of inserting a narrative loop is to play around with memory. Christopher Nolan's 2000 film *Memento* told the story of a man who has lost his memory and who lives only in the present, but who is obsessed with finding out who murdered his wife. The movie begins near the chronological end of the story – the protagonist's slaying of who he takes to be his wife's killer – and then gradually loops its way backwards, a few scenes at a time, to tease us with what really happened. Like *21 Grams*, *Memento* has been systematically chopped up and rearranged to entice a modern audience which needs more of a challenge; what it amounts to is a classic and very conventional murder-mystery zapped into cyber-realist form. Asked by an interviewer why he so often slices up his stories and rearranges them, *Memento*'s director, Christopher Nolan, paid tribute to the greater sophistication of his audience: 'I think people's

ability to absorb a fractured *mise-en-scène* is extraordinary compared to forty years ago.' Playing around with chronology to
suggest that the story is not really moving forward at all is not
new to avant-garde artists and filmmakers. As Jean-Luc
Godard famously quipped, 'a story should have a beginning,
middle and end – but not necessarily in that order'. The technique, however, is fresh to mainstream cinema. One of the
first experiments in offering up something like this for a
mainstream audience was Stanley Kubrick's 1956 film *The
Killing*, a movie about a group of gangsters and their attempt
to rob a racetrack. With its non-linear chronology and multiple points of view, *The Killing* was panned and quietly buried
by studio executives convinced that filmgoers wouldn't understand what was going on. At the time, they were probably
right.

The third sign of cyber-realist storytelling is when a story runs
to a multiplicity of disparate strands that the storyteller man-
ages to keep spinning at the same time. Hosting a variety of
different protagonists is nothing new in cinema; what is novel
is when all of those protagonists are pursuing various, parallel
goals that seem to have nothing at all in common for most of
the film. Moving between these multiple, scarcely overlapping stories forces the viewer to switch from one jarring piece
of information to another in order to make sense of it all. The
result of the decision to chop up *21 Grams* and rearrange its
chronology is that its disparate plot lines are thrown into a
crazed juxtaposition even before it becomes clear what has
happened and to whom. Another example is the fearsomely
fidgety 2005 geopolitical thriller and George Clooney vehicle,
Syriana. In the first half-hour, the viewer is introduced to a

total of six different plot lines that, at least for most of the film, seem to have nothing in common with each other. Sometimes it's enough to replay exactly the same events from the wildly different perspectives of those who were there. The hugely successful 2008 mystery thriller *Vantage Point*, for example, does nothing more than show the same twenty-three-minute action sequence – an attempted assassination of the American President – six times over, each time introducing a tantalisingly different glimpse of what might have happened. Then there is Charlie Kaufman and Michel Gondry's surprise 2004 hit, *Eternal Sunshine of the Spotless Mind*, which zigzags not only between different levels of its lead's consciousness, but between different time zones in the present, past and future. Fittingly for an audience that has grown up hitched to computers, the film turns on an attempt by its protagonists, Joel (Jim Carrey) and Clementine (Kate Winslet), to undergo a medical procedure in order to erase the memory of their failed and mutually painful relationship. Like *Memento*, the film's narrative structure is a perfect loop. It begins where it might normally end, with an between the two former lovers on a train after they have erased their memories of each other and their previous relationship. But it does something else, too. The result of superimposing different layers of Joel's consciousness on the story – his recovered memories, his observations of himself from within his memories, and the world outside his memories – is to present the story from a dizzying range of different perspectives that all happen to come from within the tortured psyche of the same character. Essential to the idea of multiplicity, as we shall see in the next chapter, is that the many different viewpoints which the story introduces us to present different versions of the same events, and don't necessarily arrive at the same kind of truth about what happened. The reason for watching *Eternal Sunshine of the Spotless Mind*, Charlie Kaufman explains, is to see what Joel thinks about his relationship with Clementine, and not what actually happened. 'You don't really know what their relationship is,' says Kaufman. 'You only know what Joel thinks about their relationship.'

The fourth and last element of cyber-realist storytelling follows from the third. The way in which a cyber-realist story brings together the different perspectives and goals of its protagonists is through random or unlikely ties, a device that often ends up framing the entire story. Holding together the messy edifice of *21 Grams*, for example, is a single accident that catapults its various characters into each other's lives. The tie that brings together the three storylines in *Pulp Fiction* is a stick-up in a diner, which both begins and ends the film's narrative loop. Thanks to a multiplicity of protagonists and a hornet's nest of random ties and connections, cyber-realist stories don't so much move forward as spread out around whole neighbourhoods, cities and beyond, pointing up the interconnectedness of just about everything. 'People lead very fragmented lives,' Alejandro Iñárritu, the director of *21 Grams*, told one journalist, justifying why he should want to tie together such different stories in the same tale: 'We can be on the cellular phone and on the computer and in many places in a short time. We are more conscious of things happening at the same time that can affect us.' In a similar way, the Oscar-winning film *Crash* features a wide range of characters from different walks of life in contemporary Los Angeles. The story proceeds to bring all of them together through an apparently random series of car accidents, shootings and hijackings. The result is to build random ties and connections between very different characters and thereby illustrate a rich and open-ended fable about racial tensions, hypocrisy and the sharply divided American class system. One last example: the title of the popular American TV show *The Wire* initially referred to a wire-tap which the Baltimore police were using to try to nail an outfit of local drug dealers, but soon became a metaphor for the premise that a wide variety of different organisations in the city were deeply and organically connected. The series started out as a cops-and-gangsters story but soon spread out to tie together different worlds that initially appeared to have little in common: street drug-dealing, the police, government and political lobbyists, schools and the media. In *The Wire*, no single character or storyline takes precedence; many are kept spinning at the same time, and its different worlds are brought together via a random or unlikely connection to illustrate how everything is quietly tied to everything else. Interviewed by the *New Yorker* in 2007, its creator David Simon insisted that *The Wire* 'was never a cop show. We were always planning to move further and further out, to build a whole city.'

The new cyber-realism and its constituent elements – the puzzle, the loop, multiplicity and the tie – allows us much more freedom to meander our way through stories in film and cinema and discover our own path. It does so, for the most part, by making us constantly adjust our expectations in response to a rich and continuous loop of jarring information. Long before the world wide web was widespread, many of the world's best novelists and film-makers – everyone from James Joyce to Salvador Dalí – were experimenting with non-traditional ways of telling stories. More recently, some novelists have become enthusiastic about the idea of literature as a

network of connections, and about a kind of non-linear storytelling that digresses rather than takes the shortest possible
route between its beginning and its end. Just before he died
in September 1985, the acclaimed Italian storyteller Italo
Calvino was working on a series of lectures about the future of
literary storytelling, which he was due to present at Harvard
University later that month. In the last lecture that he managed to complete, whose title was 'Multiplicity', Calvino
defined the novel as 'the multiplication of possibilities . . .
above all a network of connections between the events, the
people, and the things of the world'. The best novels, he
argued, were those in which 'the least thing is seen as the
centre of a network of relationships that the writer cannot
restrain himself from following, multiplying the details so
that his descriptions and digressions become infinite.
Whatever the starting point, the matter in hand spreads out
and out, encompassing ever vaster horizons, and if it were per-
mitted to go on further and further in every direction, it would
end by embracing the entire universe.'

The pedigree of this kind of panoramic storytelling can be
traced all the way back to Charles Dickens. The only thing
new here, perhaps, is the medium. One way of making sense of
these new kinds of stories is to say that they are beginning to
take on all the weight and complexity of those sumptuous,
many-layered novels much loved by the Victorians, which
seem to contain the whole world within their covers – and
which, like the box-set TV series that we huddle over our
computers to watch today, were often produced in tiny gobbets
for newspaper serialisation and consumed a little at a time. The
promise of cyber-realist storytelling is that viewers are tired of
formulaic narratives and are looking instead for richer stories

that allow them greater freedom of movement. The danger is that the audience fails to decipher any meaning in this explosion of information and perspective, that they end up going around in circles and that they are left – like those suspiciously well-preserved characters from that daft American TV series – utterly, utterly lost.

7

Multiplicity

In 2006, AOL's chief researcher, Dr Abdur Chowdhury, had a brainwave that was brilliant, but got him the sack. Given how many millions of people were typing their thoughts into AOL's search engine in search of enlightenment, he reckoned, why not post that information somewhere public and try to do something interesting with it? Even though he worked for a huge multinational, Chowdhury wanted to initiate a rare act of corporate altruism. Before he had been hired by AOL he had worked as an academic, researching electronic information and what can be done with it. He was well aware that, outside the big companies who can afford to buy it, fresh data about human behaviour was becoming incredibly difficult to come by, especially among the academic researchers who were best placed to make use of it. His plan was to gift those researchers with the freshest and most immediate data there was – a whole new set of tools with which to understand the interests and preoccupations of internet users. Naturally, there were going to be safeguards. In order to protect the privacy of AOL's customers the identifying name of each AOL user would be removed and replaced by an anonymous numerical user name. The data would be posted on an obscure web site, where only academics would be likely to come across it. Knowing what was going on in the minds of internet users, Chowdhury figured, might help technologists to design better and smarter internet search engines. More importantly, it would surely prove an enormous boon for researchers who were trying to understand human thought processes and intentions.

The website went live on 4 August 2006. Chowdhury's decision to post the data didn't reckon on the feeding frenzy that often follows the low-key release of sensitive information onto the internet. When his huge file was chanced upon and investigated by a passing internet user it was discovered to contain no less than twenty-three million search keywords for 650,000 AOL users over three months earlier that year. To the hordes of subterranean geeks and hackers who make it their mission to embarrass multinational companies, Christmas had come early. It took only three days for managers at AOL to find the file and remove it from circulation, but they were already too late. Within hours it had been pilfered by nimble internet users and pasted up all over the more anarchic corners of Cyburbia. While none of AOL's customers was directly identifiable, what made the release of the company's data so exciting was that for the first time it was possible to trace a sequence of keywords tapped into a search engine back to the individual user responsible for those searches. Even before 2006 there were search engines that would allow people to spend whole days bearing puzzled witness to the random thoughts of millions of internet users just as soon as they typed in their keywords. What was different about

AOL's data, however, was that it ascribed a number to each internet user and a time for each of their searches, allowing anyone with access to the data to follow each user's train of thought. It wasn't very long before some of those numbers were traced back to real people. Within a week a diligent reporter from the *New York Times* was able to put a name to one, a sixty-two-year-old widow from Georgia called Thelma Arnold. Over a three-month period, Arnold had typed keywords ranging from '60 single men' to 'dog that urinates on everything'. When she inputted the names of several people with the surname Arnold and the search string 'homes sold in shadow lake subdivision gwinnett county Georgia', she gave herself away. 'Those were my searches,' she admitted, when the *New York Times* reporter began to read back to her a list of her internet-transmitted thoughts. As he continued to read her guilt turned to anger. 'My goodness, it's my whole personal life,' she said. 'I had no idea somebody was looking over my shoulder.'

No one, in fact, had been looking over Thelma Arnold's shoulder, or over the shoulders of any of the hundreds of thousands of people whose most intimate thoughts had been released onto the internet. In the brouhaha over privacy and data protection that followed, during which Abdur Chowdhury was loudly fired and his research unit closed down, it was too easy to forget that everyone involved had voluntarily typed this material into a gigantic database, one that was, as a result, capable of compiling a comprehensive ledger of each of their internet-mediated thoughts just as soon they wrote them. Within days, whole websites dedicated to understanding and representing what that data meant had sprung up. The most enterprising among them went beyond simply publishing the material to analyse it and speculate as to its meaning. Some went as far as to build mini search engines which passers-by on the internet could use to mine the AOL data. One of the most popular was called AOL Stalker. Anyone who had any interest in Britney Spears, for example, could type her name into AOL Stalker and up would come a list of all of those AOL users who had searched for Britney Spears over the three month period for which search data was available. More importantly, by looking at what the anonymous searchers had typed before and after they had searched for Britney Spears, it was possible to arrive at a rough idea of the train of thought of those who were interested in finding out about the tearaway pop-star pin-up. True to the voyeuristic spirit of the internet, AOL Stalker even allowed its users to stalk the search keywords of those who were using its own search engine to stalk AOL's customers.

With entertainment possibilities like this, it is no surprise that AOL Stalker became an instant and glorious success. The man behind it, a reserved twenty-six-year-old Swede who identified himself only as Hjalmar, told me that he set it up simply to cock a snook at AOL. Just like the hippie gurus of cybernetics, Hjalmar wanted to burrow around the authorities to put information into the hands of his peers – and the very fact that a multinational like AOL wanted to withdraw that information from public consumption was reason enough for him to make sure it found an audience. The result was to make it a goldmine for voyeurs. Browsing AOL Stalker, Hjalmar admitted to me, must be very similar to looking at one's neighbours through binoculars, except that whereas before people had only a handful of people to look at, now they could stare out onto the digital minutiae of millions of other people's lives. He wasn't much interested in the material personally, he said, but, asked for an example of a popular sequence of searches filched from

AOL's data scandal, he forwarded me the data for one AOL customer whose searches had been downloaded more than fifty
thousand times. The anonymous internet user seems to be a
woman, and the three months of chronological searches that we
have for her tells us a great deal about her life and her mental
state. At the beginning of March 2006 she appears to be in the
early stages of pregnancy:

2006-03-01 18:54:10 Body fat calliper
2006-03-05 08:53:23 Curb morning sickness
2006-03-09 18:49:37 Get fit while pregnant

Two days later her mood seems to darken:

2006-03-11 03:52:01. He doesn't want the baby
2006-03-11 03:52:58. You're pregnant he doesn't want the baby

Soon things are back to normal and her enthusiasm for having
the baby returns:

2006-03-14 19:11:28. Baby names and meanings
2006-03-28 09:28:25. Maternity clothes
2006-03-29 10:01:39. Pregnancy workout videos
2006-03-29 10:12:38. Buns of steel video

It's not long, however, before she seems to be having second
thoughts:

2006-04-17 11:00:02 Abortion clinics charlotte nc
2006-04-17 11:40:22 Greater Carolinas Womens Center
2006-04-17 21:14:19 Can Christians be forgiven for abortion

2006-04-17 22:22:07 Roe vs. Wade
2006-04-18 06:50:34 Effects of abortion on fibroids
2006-04-18 15:14:03 Abortion clinic charlotte
2006-04-18 16:14:07 Symptoms of miscarriage

A few days later, she is thinking about engagement rings.

2006-04-20 16:58:37 Engagement rings

On the same day, however, abortion is still weighing on user 672368's mind:

2006-04-20 17:53:49 High-risk abortions

Two days later, the decision seems to have been made on her behalf.

2006-05-22 18:17:53 Recover after miscarriage

Only several days later her thoughts turn once again to marriage.

2006-05-06 21:22:18 www.weddingchannel.org
2006-05-26 19:32:52 Demetrios bridesmaid dresses
2006-05-27 07:25:45 Marry your live-in

Hjalmar had nudged me in the direction of the affecting and real-life story of one woman's pregnancy, her subsequent wrestle with the fact that her baby might not be wanted, and her eventual miscarriage. As the sequence of searches ends the user seems to be recovering from that miscarriage and looking forward to marriage. All of this, of course, can only be inferred. No one can really know what is going on inside the heads of internet users just from the keywords that they type, because the internet is not a complete approximation of our thought processes. All the same, the data trail that each of us leaves is awesome in its sophistication – the best of these sequences read like inchoate stories of our lives – and its potential uses are a little scary. Take another example, a user who starts off innocently thinking about doing some sewing:

2006-03-01 23:30:28 Sewing patterns
2006-03-02 00:10:17 Free sewing patterns for the triangle cup
    bathing suit
2006-03-02 00:41:23 How to make a string bikini
2006-03-04 00:26:04 How to make a bra

Ten days later, her mood has shifted abruptly and disturbingly:

2006-03-14 20:44:41 What a neck looks like after it was strangled
2006-03-14 21:38:57 Pictures of victims that have been strangled
2006-03-14 22:37:52 Pictures of murder by strangulation
2006-05-20 11:47:43 What is manila rope used for
2006-05-20 14:07:42 Brown paper bags cops use for evidence
2006-05-21 12:49:21 Rope to use to hog tie someone

Is she planning a murder? The evidence suggests that she is. Only towards the end of her online soliloquy does it appear that she is simply doing some research into the death of JonBenét Ramsey, the six-year-old beauty queen whose unsolved 1996 murder is one of the most enduring mysteries in recent American history, when she searches for a television interview with Ramsey's parents.

2006-05-26 15:12:45 CNN interview John and Patsy Ramsey

Despite their oblique and fragmentary nature, our internet-mediated thoughts are increasingly considered admissible as evidence in courts of law. In November 2005 prosecutors in a North Carolina murder trial, in which the victim had been strangled, unveiled the apparently damning evidence, extracted from a seized personal computer, that the defendant had typed 'neck', 'snap', 'break' and 'hold' into Google at around the same time as the murder. This evidence was taken seriously, and it helped the prosecution to win a conviction. Beyond the obvious concerns about privacy and the nature of intentionality, the availability of information like this raises a number of questions. Marshall McLuhan's idea all those years ago was that the tools we use to send and retrieve information end up influencing the way that we think, and that those tools were going to change radically with the arrival of a continuous electrical information loop. The elementary truth of this will be recognised by anyone who has ever approached a word processor to gather their thoughts. Even before we spent vast tracts of our time using the internet, many of us were unknowingly learning the habit of writing on computers in very different ways to how our parents used to write on paper – no longer producing a linear series of neatly ordered thoughts but a cat's cradle of ideas, insights and suggestions that we would then go on to rearrange into something closer to a traditional story or argument.

In the last chapter, we saw how the time we spend on an electronic information loop is affecting the kinds of stories that we want to listen to. In the same way, it is entirely possible that the ready availability of information on Google is affecting our neural circuitry and the way that we form and order our thoughts. The relationship between our brain and our internet search box is, after all, a whirring electronic information loop like any other. What is missing in AOL's data, of course, is any sense of how the user's train of thought proceeds after each internet search. Unless we are very lucky and get where we want to go with one click of our mouse, each keyword search is only the point of departure for a long and winding adventure that takes us deep into Cyburbia, hopping from hyperlink to hyperlink as we go. Only after all that, armed with information as feedback from our search, do we loop back to the internet search box and start again.

The most striking thing about the huge database of musings made visible in these web searches is their propensity for sudden and unpredictable twists and turns. The electronic information loop that exists between our brain and our internet search box interrupts our thinking and decision-making cycle, spurring us to think through and act on different impulses and musings with much greater agility than we would have been capable of before. The time that we spend hitched to Google's information loop teaches us, just as Norbert Wiener predicted it would, to behave like highly responsive cybernetic steersmen – zigzagging between a multiplicity of trains of thought in response to a constant stream of information and feedback, and often holding various of those trains of thought in our head at the same time. Though academic studies find it difficult to measure, the light-footed way in which we dart through Google's information loop might also be affecting the way that we think when we leave our search engines behind. Left unchecked, it might affect our ability to concentrate on longer pieces of writing without switching our attention away somewhere else.

But what do we know about where our Google-mediated journey through Cyburbia takes us? The streams of consciousness that we tap into its search box, of course, are rarely evidence of our most considered thoughts and reflections. Instead, they hold up a mirror to our disordered psyche. The direct and immediate plugging of internet search words into our brains via Google's information loop means that what comes out the other end often reads like a kind of electronic unconscious: a whirling gush of thoughts, desires, and impulses which lacks direction and focus, and which, just like the way we use Google itself, can sometimes spill over into the rest of our lives. Take one last sequence of searches unearthed from AOL's treasure trove. User X seems to be a woman unhappy with her partner and contemplating an affair with someone she has hooked up with on the internet. Dipping her toe in the water, she starts by searching out some statistics:

2006-03-04 14:30 How many online romances lead to sex

At the same time, she is looking for information to help her cope with her partner:

2006-04-07 09:19 How to deal with self-absorbed braggers

The day after, she has decided to go through with meeting the man she has been flirting with on the internet.

2006-04-08 19:33 How to deal with nervousness when meeting a new person

A month later, the deed seems to have been done:

2006-05-07 10:04 I cheated on my spouse

Very soon, however, things are beginning to go awry.

2006-05-08 20:58 Person I had an affair with is trying to contact
me again
2006-05-12 21:11 I took cyber sex to a physical level and it was
a mistake

In a sinister development, she soon begins to suspect that her online meanderings are being spied on by her partner.

2006-05-015 14:52 How can you tell if your spouse put spyware
on your computer?

It isn't long before she becomes upset, and sends a silent howl of frustration out into the ether.

2006-05-29 09:24 Why are affairs so complicated?

Only two minutes later, however, she is thinking about buying new furniture:

2006-05-29 09:26 Basset furniture store Houston Texas

The next day, she decides that she will avoid men who spend too much time on the internet.

2006-05-30 13:41 Something wrong with men that like to spend
a lot of time on online chatting

And that she needs to seek help for her own dependence on the net:

2006-05-30 18:26 Treating computer addiction

Feeling guilty, she is also, perhaps, resolving to be nicer to the man in her life:

2006-05-31 23:27 How to make a man long with desire for you

The many trains of thought that seem to depart when we type words into search engines, together with our propensity for switching between them, are only one way in which our attention is pulled in different directions by the time we spend on an electronic information loop. Think, for example, about what happens when we sit down at our work terminals or home computers. On our computer desktops are a variety of different applications and documents that demand our attention and which we juggle as best we can. Before we have even got around to our e-mail or the world wide web, the windows we open on our computers tempt us to pay attention to many different things at once. When we hook up to the internet and open up a window on to Cyburbia, things become yet more complicated. The continuous loop of information with which we engage our mouse and our computer, and which Norbert Wiener predicted would one day animate cybernetic man with a steady stream of instructions, no longer comes only from a machine but from each and every person whom we are in contact with via the internet. Through web applications such as instant messenger, e-mail and social networking sites we have opened that information loop to encompass communication with all our many electronic ties. We are now faced with a new kind of electronic information loop that demands our rapid response and adjustment not to a computer or a video game but to everyone we know. If previously we imagined our cybernetic self as an anti-aircraft gunner up against a single enemy pilot, now we confront a whole squadron.

One result of all this has been to change utterly the role that electronic media plays in our lives, especially among teenagers and young adults. The teenager who spends hours in her bedroom at her computer will have multiple different windows open onto Cyburbia at the same time. Some of those will represent different information trails she has followed on her internet browser; all will be open and 'tabbed' so that each train of thought remains active and can be returned to in an instant. Other windows will look out onto conversations that she is having on instant messenger. Since her conversation partner may be entering and leaving the room and shifting between different tasks, conversations will progress in fits and starts and have a patchwork quality – questions will be asked but not answered, conversations will go off in multiple directions, sometimes she and her conversation partner will appear to be talking past one other. The conversation will be complicated by the fact that she will usually be talking to more than one person at the same time. As she moves in and out of those different conversational threads, she will constantly be switching tone and register. Sometimes she will even be trying on different identities, presenting herself differently – a glamorous mature woman, a cheeky schoolgirl vamp, even, just to confuse any lecherous old men she happens to encounter, as a cranky old pensioner called Bob. Very often she will have the TV on at the same time, but she will not really be watching it.

Instead she will use it as colourful electronic wallpaper, background entertainment while she switches between a range of more pressing tasks. That television has been pushed into the background by a new generation who prefer to hang out in Cyburbia is already well established. Over four out of five British under-thirties, a study published in the autumn of 2007 discovered, routinely do something else while watching TV; among fifteen-to-seventeen-year-olds, the figure was as high as 86 per cent.

For a young woman like this, playfully trying on different identities in the safety of her bedroom, it is sometimes difficult to know whether the medium is affecting her or the other way round. It is not hard to see, however, why rapidly responding and reacting to a stream of electronic messages sent by her peers should be more pressing and more intense an experience than sitting on a sofa watching TV. Television, according to a 2008 report, has now been overthrown by mobile phones and the internet as the most important medium among Britain's teenagers; more British sixteen-to-nineteen-year-olds told surveyors that they couldn't do without a mobile phone than said they couldn't do without a TV. So many Belgian teenagers are leaving their mobiles on at night, a study from that country discovered, that the noise of arriving text messages was affecting the sleep of nearly half of the country's sixteen-year-olds. Neither is it just young people in the West who are in thrall to a continuous loop of information sent via their peers. Alarmed by a survey suggesting that nearly 14 per cent of Chinese teens were hooked on online games, in 2007 the Chinese government banned the opening of new cybercafés and issued a law limiting the amount of time that children and teenagers can spend playing games in such establishments. Even harsher are conditions for online gamers in South Korea, where about 30 per cent of children are alleged to be at risk from addiction to online games. Hundreds of treatment centres have been set up to encourage the afflicted to kick their habit. Lured or dragged into one of those treatment centres, goggle-eyed young Koreans are forced to endure group therapy sessions or courses in drumming and pottery.

Today's teenagers and young adults are native to Cyburbia. Having grown up hitched to its online information loop, they find it a welcoming place and spend time there as if it were a second home. Neither are us adults immune to the visceral pull of the place. Stories of our attachment to rapid electronic response abound: of people firing off rude or insulting e-mails without allowing themselves time to think, or of people whiling away whole evenings chatting or flirting with many different strangers at the same time, or of people staying up late into the night to bid against each other on eBay. Sometimes the pressure of that stream of information is literally breathtaking. When we sit down to check our e-mail after a long absence many of us instinctively hold our breath as if we had just dived underwater. Thanks to mobile e-mail gadgets like the BlackBerry, however, long absences from our e-mail are getting more difficult to engineer. BlackBerry started out as a business tool in 1997 before inveigling its way into the rest of our lives; its inventor, Mike Lazaridis, has called it a 'remote-control to your life'. But just who is controlling whom? Most of BlackBerry's twenty million users around the world set up their devices either to vibrate or to wink them a red LED alert at each and every incoming e-mail. According to a study published in July 2007, six out of ten American BlackBerry users check their e-mails in bed. Two out of five told researchers they kept their 'crackberries' nearby while they slept so they could hear incoming mail, and a similar proportion said they had replied to e-mails in the middle of the night, as well as admitting to sneaking off the occasional e-mail while driving their cars.

In March 2008 the *American Journal of Psychiatry* took account of some of this international evidence to announce that it had added 'internet addiction' – excessive use of the internet followed by periods of anguished withdrawal – to its official list of mental disorders. Even though the stream of information that comes from our myriad ties is much more pressing than other kinds of media, it is not very helpful to think of users of electronic media as addicts, even if, as we saw in the thoughts of user X, that's often how they think about themselves. Much better to imagine all this as the corollary of a new kind of self that many of us now inhabit: one who craves being in the information loop via e-mail, text message and online networks at all times, and who is continually opening that information loop and then vainly trying to slam it shut by firing off rapid bursts of feedback. When inhabitants of Cyburbia return there compulsively to check for updates, they are not only trying to be more efficient and more productive, but to ward off a persistent fear of falling out of the loop.

But there is something else here too. To properly stay in the loop, we are forced to continually adjust ourselves to the many demands of our electronic ties. The teenager in her bedroom is not the only one whose attention is pulled apart by switching between different digital media. Three quarters of twenty-to-thirty-four-year-olds, according to an exhaustive survey produced by the British communications watchdog Ofcom in 2008, now regularly use their mobile while they sit in front of the television, while more than a third of British twenty-five- to-forty-four-year-olds routinely watch TV with one eye on the internet. In a memorable phrase, Linda Stone, a former Microsoft researcher, has argued that this constant switching between different electronic ties or connections has turned us into people defined by our 'continuous partial attention' to the world around us. Being a busy node on a many-headed information network and rapidly switching between its different channels, Stone told me, has in the last decade become an end in itself – something that we do not only because it makes us work harder or better, but because it fits very well with the kind of people that we aspire to be. Paying continuous partial attention to many different streams of information is very different from what we think of as multi-tasking or simply doing lots of different things at once. Multi-tasking, she says, was only about doing things faster and more efficiently, whereas paying continuous partial attention is motivated by a more playful desire to have an active role in our network of connections and not to miss anything. Indeed, when we pay continuous partial attention 'we are always in high alert . . . this artificial sense of constant crisis is more typical of continuous partial attention than it is of multi-tasking'. This sense of an impending crisis that sends us back, again and again, to our electronic information loop is curiously in keeping with Norbert Wiener's original vision of a cybernetic system. Remember that Wiener, whose world-view had been thrown out of kilter by the devastation and barbarism of the Second World War, had come to see society as a giant messaging system constantly on the verge of destroying itself, a system that could only be kept in check by the planting of myriad information feedback loops with which to monitor its operation. Without those feedback loops disorder would surely engulf the whole system and hurl it toward its inevitable collapse. Raised in the image of Wiener's cybernetics, it should come as no surprise that we are compelled to check our mobile phones and our e-mail as if the world depended on it.

But what does it do to us to constantly switch our attention between different communication channels? Our understanding of neuroscience is still in its relative infancy, but recent advances in the field have made us more deeply aware of the astonishing malleability of the brain and its adaptability to its environment. We are born with hundreds of billions of neurons, and those neurons are constantly forming connections in response to new experiences: from the earliest years of our childhood, everything we think or do changes the relationship between them and helps make us the people we become. The part of the brain whose job it is to deal with signals and stimuli is known as the prefrontal cortex, and is situated at the front of the skull. While it is difficult to completely isolate functions to different parts of the brain – like an orchestra or a football team, it is best thought of as a group of players acting in indivisible concert – the prefrontal cortex is known to play a highly significant role in organising our short-term decision making. Neuroscientists have known about this function for decades, and they call it executive control. Think of it as the brain's secretary or chairperson; its job is to plan ahead and make decisions, to take account of all the immediate messages and stimuli that come its way, rank their importance and make sure we focus only on those which are most pressing. The ability to respond to stimuli is crucial for our development. When someone is subjected to a frontal lobotomy – those unfortunate

patients in *One Flew Over the Cuckoo's Nest*, for instance – their
prefrontal cortex is damaged, which is why they often appear
dull and unresponsive. On the other hand, rapid reaction to
any and every stimulus can be self-defeating. When we walk
down the street and hear a loud noise our natural and immediate instinct is to look around. If, however, we reacted to
every single aural and visual stimulus which crossed our path
we would become incapable of progressing with any sense
of purpose. The job of our executive controller, then, is to
filter incoming messages and to exercise a little discipline and
restraint. Executive control evolves relatively late in life, which
is the reason why some small children are not very good at
it, and its development plays a vital role in readying kids for
school and later life. Back in the sixties, a psychologist at
Stanford University called Michael Mischel offered a marshmallow each to a group of hungry four-year-olds, but promised
that he would double their allowance to two marshmallows if
they could wait for five minutes while he ran an errand and
came back. About one-third of the group downed the single
marshmallow straight away, while the rest waited for Mischel to
return. Years later, when the children had become adults,
Mischel interviewed them again. What he discovered was that
those early habits died hard: those who resisted the temptation
of the first offer were more successful in life and career, while
those who succumbed tended to be more stubborn and indecisive, and to have trouble subordinating their immediate
impulses to long-term goals.

The time that we spend in Cyburbia teaches us to respond
rapidly to messages and stimuli just as soon as they come our
way. But what if there is a price to be paid in return? What if
wading through a constant stream of messages from our

electronic ties ends up placing an insuperable burden on our executive controller, so much so that it compromises our ability to pay attention to the task at hand? There's no doubt that trying to react to many different streams of information at the same time tends to slow us down and increases our susceptibility to making mistakes. A very literal warning of the errors that can result came early in 2008, when Brick Lane, the fashionable east London street, announced that it was henceforth padding its lampposts as a preventive measure against the growth of 'talk and text' injuries that were maiming thousands of the young hipsters who amble along it. More surprising, perhaps, is that it is not necessarily the technology-savvy young who are better at avoiding these creeping errors. An ongoing research project into this area at Oxford University's Institute for the Future of the Mind asked two different groups of subjects – one between the ages of eighteen and twenty-one, the other between thirty-five and thirty-nine – to perform a simple intelligence test of translating images into numbers. The test only lasted ninety seconds, but when both groups were interrupted by a phone call, text message or an instant message the results surprised the researchers. The younger group, as expected, performed better than their elders when there were no interruptions. When both groups were interrupted, however, the older ones matched the youngsters for both speed and the accuracy with which they completed the test. The findings successfully flip on their head the stereotype that younger people, who have spent a lifetime in Cyburbia, are necessarily better at doing and communicating lots of different things at once. In fact, what they suggest is that the ability to keep lots of things on the boil comes with maturity, and that young people are still learning those skills. Though it is difficult to say for definite, it may be that the ability of very young people to prioritise their tasks – their internal secretary – might end up hampered by the constant interruptions that flow from their dependence on communications gadgetry. Those who are too used to the richly visual environments of computers and video games, according to Jonathan Sharples of the Institute for the Future of the Mind, might find that when they move to less visually stimulating environments or are left with their own thoughts, their ability to control their train of thought doesn't work as well as it should.

Neuroscience, however, is not the only way to understand what spending time as a live node on a many-headed network might be doing to our brains. Like many psychologists, Adam Cox, a clinical psychologist based in Rhode Island who works to understand how children use communications devices, prefers to think about it using the idea of our 'working memory' – our ability to hold concepts or notions in our short-term memory long enough to learn them. 'Working memory' is an extension of the computer metaphor which, as we saw in Chapter 4, began to influence our understanding of just about everything in the sixties and seventies. When we buy a new computer, what we want to know is how much memory it has for storing bits of information. The other thing we want to know about is its processing power – its ability to juggle lots of different programs or applications at once, or to have lots of different windows open at the same time. Human working memory, Cox argues, can be compared to a computer's processing power. It is the reason why we can remember a number of different pieces of information at the same time – think of that time you tried to remember the digits of someone's telephone number, for example, by constant repeating it to brand each number into your memory. Given a task to perform or to understand, our mental processing power goes to work on learning how to do it and then transfers that knowledge into our long-term memory.

Our working memory is much more responsive to stimuli from our environment than our long-term memory. Cox believes that the delivery of a continuous stream of messages might well help to stimulate the brain, making us better at doing lots of different things at once. That same part of the brain, however, is likely to become strained if we make too many demands on it. Get interrupted too often and the danger is that our ability to learn things properly might be impaired. In other words, beyond a certain point the productivity bonus that we get from responding to many different streams of information on an electronic information loop at the same time levels off then begins to slow us down. All this matters because managing multiple activities, tasks and information streams is now considered to be a basic characteristic of working life. When researchers at the University of California shadowed fourteen office workers over seven months in 2004 to see how they used technology they discovered that, on average, their subjects got three minutes of work done before being diverted or interrupted and having to switch tasks. When they did get around to resuming work on the project from which they had been distracted it took an average of twenty-five minutes for that to happen. If multiple other windows had been opened in the meantime, sometimes people even found it tricky to remember which document they had been working on before they had been interrupted. Sometimes the fall-off in productivity can be precipitous. In 2005, for example, researchers at the Institute of Psychiatry in London gave two groups of people intelligence tests and had one group check electronic messages on their mobiles while taking it. The interrupted group turned out to lose an average of ten points on the IQ test. Even worse, their scores compared rather unfavourably with the results of a different test in which the subjects were allowed to smoke cannabis. Using new communications gizmos to multi-task, shrieked the newspaper headlines that followed, was worse for us than getting high.

Just like the time that we spend on Google's information loop, then, responding to a stream of messages on an electronic information loop intervenes in our normal thinking and decision-making cycle – and if we are not careful, it can knock us off balance. Before we convict our computers and mobiles of turning everyone into fidgety stoners with the attention span of baby goldfish, however, it helps to get a little perspective. At least for many of us, work doesn't exercise our minds a great deal. Unless your job is writing symphonies or performing complex medical operations, it is highly unlikely that you need to give it your undivided attention all of the time. Often it is only because many of us are under-stimulated in the first place that we offer ourselves up to a never-ending communications loop of e-mail chatter, texts and instantaneous updates from social networking sites. In an intriguing detail included as an afterthought to their study, the University of California researchers noted that the workers they shadowed interrupted themselves just as often as they were interrupted by other people. When I asked Gloria Mark, one of the researchers behind the study, why people were so keen to interrupt themselves her answer was that people have become so conditioned to being interrupted that interrupting themselves might be a way of claiming back some control of their lives.

Perhaps the analogy between the time that we spend switching between tasks and the experience of being stoned isn't such a bad one after all. Just as Linda Stone hypothesised, our enthusiasm for paying continuous partial attention is not at all about trying to do things more efficiently. The reason why many of us are so keen to move through a range of tasks and connections and constantly jump around between them is that we have simply come to appreciate it for its own sake. Having grown up threaded to video games, computers, mobile phones and the internet, the idea of being an active node on an information network has become so important to us that we often experience it as a kind of light relief. If sometimes our brains cannot cope and everything ends in a muddle, maybe that is exactly what we are looking for – the space to log in, zone out and idle away a little time in Cyburbia.

Think once more about AOL's misplaced data file and the story of user X. Dizzy with anticipation at the prospect of consummating her online affair, user X seems to have become a little vain. Take this twenty-eight minute snapshot of her internet-mediated train of thought:

2006-04-26 18:21 How can I make my hair look thicker and fuller?
2006-04-26 18:22 How can a fair skinned light haired light eyed person brighten up their face?
2006-04-26 18:34 How can I bring out light eyes?
2006-04-26 18:35 How can I bring out blue eyes with makeup?
1006-04-26 18:47 What color do blondes look good in?
2006-04-26 18:49 What color clothes do blondes look good in?

Our internet search box is not only a confessional booth to which we give up our secret desires. It is our oracle too. Scroll through the mass of fragmented thoughts in AOL's search data and it is littered with who, what, how or why questions like those asked by user X. But to whom are her questions addressed? The search box she typed her questions into was owned by AOL, but the information trail was far longer than that. In 2002 AOL entered into a long-term agreement to have its searches powered by Google, which means that searches typed into AOL's search engine were immediately forwarded to Google as soon as they were asked. User 711391's questions, together with the information trail she took through the range of answers presented to her, went straight to a massive farm of computer servers owned or controlled by Google.

That user X's questions found their way into the hands of Google is not unusual, because three out of five internet searches anywhere in the world are answered by the company. Google's mission statement commits it to organising the world's information and rendering it accessible and useful. This is easier said than done. Google's worthy ambition of digitising all the world's books, for example, is a complex project that will likely take many decades to complete, even if it isn't scuppered by the opposition of everyone from authors to publishers to advertising agencies. In the meantime, what Google does so well is to bring everyone within range of the internet into a fluid and chaotic global conversation – one that is constantly being refreshed by the questions and opinions of each and every one of them. Think about what happens when you hear a couple of bars of a song or lines from a poem but can't remember what it is. Or the time you met someone at a party but forgot to get their details. Perhaps even the time you completely forgot the spelling of an obscure word. Rather than consult a trusted, traditional source of information or ask around, there is a good chance that, just like user X, you drifted to a little internet search box in search of answers. In turn, the chances are that that search box led straight to Google.

With this in mind, some technology boosters have been arguing that Google and sites like it are becoming the main-spring of a new kind of global consciousness or global brain. By 2015, according to Kevin Kelly, the founding editor of *Wired* magazine and the sometime editor of the *Whole Earth Catalog*, the internet as we know it will have vanished and in its place will have arisen a 'globe-spanning artificial con-sciousness'. The argument is a familiar one. Half a century ago, as we saw in Chapter 3, Marshall McLuhan predicted that, where technologies had previously acted to support and extend our bodies, the final phase of our reliance as extensions of ourselves would take place when all of our brains were hooked up via an electrical network into a single and all-pow-erful global brain. Many think that his prediction is now on the verge of coming true. Think again about how Google works. When Google emerged as a giant from the ruins of the dotcom boom, it did so because ordinary people took to search-ing through a constantly shifting web of information created, linked and ranked by their peers in a never-ending feedback loop. Long before its competitors, Google's knack was to realise that people navigated their way though Cyburbia not by infor-mation per se, but by examining the relationship between bits of information – in other words, how many other people found that information worth a look.

Does all this add up to a transcendent global consciousness, the collective knowing which McLuhan thought might eventually tie us together and make us aware of our common humanity? A better analogy can be found by retracing McLuhan's steps back to Norbert Wiener, from whom he borrowed the vision of the coming cybernetic age. It was Wiener who had been one of the first to think of the human brain as a cybernetic instrument and to compare its operation with that of an early computer. Excited by the possibilities suggested by his cybernetic metaphor, Wiener had begun to imagine that both brains and computers worked to correct their mistakes and malfunctions in similar ways. The perfect cybernetic electrical machine or computer would make good its errors by simultaneously referring every operation to two or three different computers, whose answers were then measured against one another, collated and a majority verdict chosen. The brain surely worked in much the same way. Like the computing machine, Wiener posited in his book *Cybernetics*, 'the brain probably works on a variant of the famous principle expounded by Lewis Carroll in "The Hunting of the Snark": "What I tell you three times is true".'

Wiener's analogy between the workings of the brain and that of a primitive computer network was entirely speculative; as he readily admitted at the time, it had no basis at all either in neuroscience or psychiatry. Sixty years later his account of the way in which a primitive computer network works to correct its mistakes seems an uncannily perspicacious account of how we use the 'networked brain' offered to us by search engines. When we sit lazily typing words into Google, what we want is often not an objectively correct answer but to browse some of the most frequently cited answers as they bubble up from our Google-powered global conversation. When user X asks what colour blondes look good in, the chances are that she is not looking for the expert opinion of a professional stylist. More likely she wants to tap into a conversation of her peers, to canvass what people think and why they think it before she makes her decision. It's even possible that she typed in that particular combination of words because she thought they might stand the best chance of catching the attention of her peers. In the same way, when we type the lyrics of a song or a poem, or the name of a person, into Google we are less likely to be seeking a purportedly objective source of information in a newspaper or encyclopaedia than in the algorithmic echo of a multiplicity of different voices, from which we then try to make up our own mind. The truth of this was discovered by Google itself in 2002 when it offered its users the chance to pose their questions to expert researchers who had been screened by its employees. Google Answers was a miserable, unpopular flop for the company, and was quietly binned four years later.

The inhabitants of this place called Cyburbia, as we saw in Chapter 5, stubbornly prefer to route around the influence of gatekeepers and authorities in favour of a conversation with their peers. The result, in many industries, has been to throw up a ready alternative to many hierarchies based on information and expertise, and subject everything possible to a new kind of peer-review system based on the opinion of masses of ordinary punters. The precipitous collapse of the habit of newspaper reading among young adults, for example, has not thus far been compensated for by their gravitation towards newspaper websites. Among those young Britons who do not read a paper regularly, a large-scale survey reported at the beginning of 2008, only 3 per cent regularly consult a newspaper website. In another poll published early in 2008, it was reported that more British people trusted the news they managed to scavenge from online sources than the stuff they were being fed by newspapers. What they are doing, presumably, is trying their luck with the many different opinions of their online peers. A survey of entertainment habits published in May 2007 found that Americans now consider user reviews on websites their most valuable source of information when it comes to planning an evening out. Respondents added that they trusted those peer reviews much more than those of the professional critics they might encounter in newspapers and magazines; they were even more likely to check out user reviews online than to canvass the opinion of a knowledgeable friend.

But how exactly do we go about making up our minds in Cyburbia? Some of us will trust the first source of information that Google serves up. Most, however, will take the trouble to browse through two or three. Like nodes on Wiener's primitive computer network, we are referring their question to two or three popular sources of information, collating their different opinions and then arriving at a verdict. Just as the network theorists predicted, we are taking a step back to map the web of connections between different bits of information to see where it leads us. In the same way that Facebook tries to make us into cartographers of the many different ties between the people we know, as we saw in Chapter 5, the time we spend on Google turns us into cartographers of information, tracing relationships and assembling connections in the ether to see whether it adds up to anything we can rely on.

Take one last example. For some years now the modus operandi of the online encyclopedia Wikipedia has been the subject of sniping between enthusiasts for the internet and devotees of more traditional ways of doing things. Thus far Wikipedia has fought its corner on the basis of the veracity of its entries. An encyclopaedia that allows anyone to change most of its entries at will, however, is playing a dangerous game when it allows itself to stand or fall on the basis of the absolute accuracy of its material. It also fails to do justice to an important ingredient of its appeal. People are moved to browse Wikipedia because they find a range of different and sometimes inconsistent voices and opinions there, which they can try to cross-check against each other and the sources that come with them. Just like Google and Facebook, Wikipedia makes us into map-makers, constantly and enthusiastically orienting ourselves and getting our coordinates in an effort to assess the value of the information we encounter. If sometimes we fail to get our bearings and take a wrong turning, that simply goes with the territory.

Of course, wrong turns made in Cyburbia can pay unexpected dividends. They can lead us to bump into information we didn't even know we were looking for, and can encourage our natural curiosity and thirst for discovery. Placing too much store on directions encountered in Cyburbia, however, can have real and damaging consequences. Those of us who idle away our time neurotically searching our own name – so-called 'ego-surfing' – are not just indulging in an act of unconscionable vanity. We are also anxious about what might be being said about us there. We have every reason to be, because information about us has a habit of turning up on blogs, chatrooms and social networking sites. Sometimes this is information that we would prefer to remain hidden: often it is laden with innuendo, malice or is simply untrue. No matter; in thrall to

our instantaneous online information loop we are tempted to
rely on it. The number of hits a person chalks up on Google,
for example, is increasingly seen as an easy indicator of their
popularity or their professional standing. At its worst, this
attachment to asking questions of our internet search box
recreates the stifling paranoia of traditional village life in
which someone could be damned by little more than a whisper.
A survey of one hundred American business recruiters in 2006
revealed that nearly four-fifths of them resort to search engines
when hiring new staff; more than a third had rejected a candidate on the basis of unverified information they had come
across in Cyburbia.

This picture of us as map-makers feeling our way through
Cyburbia is very far from the transcendent, all-knowing global
consciousness that Marshall McLuhan predicted our global
information network would grow up into. Perhaps the best
way to think about it is to admit that his global village hasn't
turned out quite the way he planned. The mistake that the
gurus of cybernetics made was to imagine that masses of electronic information could on their own substitute for human
consciousness or the real accumulation of knowledge. It was
always a bit much to ask that, by hooking ourselves up to an
electronic information loop and canvassing the opinions of
formless humanity, we would become aware of our obligations
to each other on a global scale.

McLuhan and the other high priests of cybernetics were
right about one thing, though. There is something awesomely
fascinating about what all this electronic chatter can tell us
about ourselves. The hodgepodge of thoughts, desires and
impulses that tumble out when we sit in front of our internet

search box tends to short-circuit our rational selves – to mirror and even exacerbate the untidy and directionless clutter of our psyche. It should hardly be surprising that what comes out the other end looks less like a new, enlightened global conscious-ness than a constantly updated printout of our collective psyche – a kind of electronic id. On its own it doesn't make much sense, but join up the dots and it makes for a uniquely powerful way of tapping into our collective mood that goes right under the radar of more traditional measures, and which is proving an unimaginable asset for those who are rich and clever enough to exploit it.

Here again Google is leading the way. At the beginning of 2008 I sat at a table in the company's plush new London offices and was shown how to use Google Trends, one of the many tools to emerge from its laboratory, to compare the numbers of people who searched for Barack Obama versus those who searched for Hillary Clinton during their race to be the Democratic Party's nomination for the 2008 American presi-dential election. Google executives are careful not to make any claims for this information beyond its ability to indicate public curiosity and public interest. Looking at the peaks and troughs of support and comparing public interest in the two over time, however, it was easy to chart very accurately the rise in public fascination with Obama and the waning of interest in Clinton. Given the symbiotic relationship between our fragmented thought processes and the words that we end up typing into internet search engines, what comes out looks like an eerily immediate chronicle of the public mood.

Google is not the only company mapping the relationship between bits of information in Cyburbia as a means of tapping into our electronic id. While we stare out of our computer

windows onto Cyburbia, it is easy to forget who is staring
back at us. Many of the same authorities and institutions that
we thought we had left behind when we migrated to Cyburbia
have quietly become peeping toms, and spend a great deal of
time monitoring the traffic there and thinking about how they
can turn it to their own advantage. There are now, for example,
several hundred million blogs in Cyburbia. Most of them are
very dull. Just like the information hoovered up by Google,
their value lies less in what they have to say than in the relationships between them in the dense thicket of links that
connects them to other blogs in a constantly shifting global
chatter box. Big companies have not been shy to use all this
information to find out what people are saying about them
behind their backs or simply to get inside the heads of their
customers. Major financial investors and the security services,
too, are investing heavily in automated systems that trawl
through this kind of electronic chatter and make sense of it.

In a place where so much effort has been expended on routing around the control of the authorities, it seems ironic that
many of our innermost thoughts and impulses should end up
collected on anonymous banks of privately owned computer
servers, there to be bought by the highest bidder. That, however, was only the beginning. With all this traffic coursing
through Cyburbia, some organisations back in the real world
were contemplating doing more than simply monitoring it
and trying to steer it in their direction. Impressed by all this
energy and activity, not a few were tempted to open up their
own decision-making loop and invite the inhabitants of
Cyburbia to have a say in what they do. As we shall see in the
following chapter, that was going to prove a riskier strategy
altogether.

8

Feedback

At the beginning of 2008 the hottest ticket in London's crowded Theatreland was a world away from all those grand, ornate museums of theatre to which tourists flock in the West End. You could buy a ticket for *The Masque of the Red Death* via one of London's top theatres, the National, but if you wanted to see it you had to trek five kilometres south-west and spend an evening in a creaking, ailing old Victorian venue called Battersea Arts Centre. Over the six months of its extended run, forty thousand people were happy to make the journey.

The Masque of the Red Death wasn't your average trip to the theatre. Strictly speaking, it wasn't even a play at all. To the uninitiated it sounded like a theatrical adaptation of Edgar Allen Poe's Gothic short story of the same name, but that didn't do anything to prepare audiences for what was about to befall them. On the evening I went, the queue outside was full of beautifully turned-out, gleefully expectant young couples.

On arrival we were handed an eerie-looking white mask and a black cloak. Split up into small groups, we were then ushered into an ante-chamber by a shifty-looking mistress of ceremonies who invited us to make our own way around a series of rooms laid out in hues inspired by Poe's brand of American Gothic. The whole of what had formerly been Battersea Town Hall had been lovingly transformed into a den of inspired seediness. Candles flickered in the darkness, stuffed foxes glared emptily at passers-by and black-clad ushers and extravagantly dressed wenches prowled around so unassumingly that it was often difficult to distinguish audience from performers. In a giant hallway a couple fought passionately as they tumbled down a marble staircase; in a bedroom, two lovers engaged in a torrid play-fight on a four-poster bed; in a cavernous banqueting hall a lavish dinner party slid into a noisy, bacchanalian orgy. For those thirsty theatregoers who could find it, there was even a bar where they could hide out and knock back a drink.

The problem was that, amid all this finery, it was maddeningly difficult to figure out what was actually going on. Rather than presenting a single adaptation of Poe's short story, the producers had chosen to chop up a selection of different Poe stories and sprinkle their fragments liberally around the different rooms and open spaces of Battersea Arts Centre so that the audience could make their own way through them. As people strolled around the idea was that they would carve out a journey that was uniquely their own. To those who were used to following traditional theatrical dramas from beginning to end, all this must have seemed very strange. That was part of the point. Even more than the critical plaudits or those enviable audience figures, what impressed people about

The Masque of the Red Death was how many young people it attracted in a genre more usually patronised by an older crowd. With plenty of experience of playing an active part in an information loop, this restless audience of young adults saw a flicker of self-recognition in the premise that theatrical performance could be a two-way street and that they, the audience, could be allowed more involvement in the theatre that they saw.

The theatre company behind all of this, Punchdrunk, was canny enough to know the reasons for its success. Its production was not quite as freewheeling as its audience liked to think. Visitors were being given license to roam around as they wished, but they were also being gently manipulated through a detailed and highly controlled series of set pieces. No wonder, then, that the director likened this kind of theatre to a game of hide and seek. And that wasn't all. Despite all the careful insistence that each of us choose our own path around the place, it was striking how much we in the audience tended to stick together. In search of cues, many of us took to darting this way and that, following a hurtling harlequin and then doubling back on ourselves to give chase to a distraught dandy. At one stage I was nearly knocked to the ground by a stampede of my fellow theatregoers on the tail of a particularly buxom wench.

Many years before all those thousands of theatregoers trooped off to Battersea to wander around a cold building, Marshall McLuhan found himself intrigued by a similar phenomenon. McLuhan had been reading with awestruck fascination the recently published work of Professor John Wilson of London University's African Institute. Wilson was just back from Africa, where he had been using short films to teach villagers techniques for better sanitation and the treatment of waste. What interested McLuhan about Wilson's written reports was his account of the way that the villagers reacted to the unfamiliar experience of watching films. Wilson discovered that, since they lacked the experience of following linear narratives, they also lacked the ability to detach themselves from the different elements of the film. So deeply involved were the African villagers in what was going on on screen that they were unable to focus on the film as a whole. As a result, and unlike Western audiences, they refused to remain rigidly passive when they were asked to watch it. If a chicken passed through the frame and exited the other side, for example, the villagers wanted to know what had happened to it and where it had gone. With this in mind, the academics began to think up opportunities for greater audience participation. The African teachers hired to introduce the films were encouraged to improvise so as to help involve the audience in the story. If, for example, a character in the film began to sing a song, the audience was invited to join in.

McLuhan's interest in the viewing habits of African villagers came about because of his conviction that Western society was about to go back to the future. Since electrical technology tends to forge a more intense bond between viewer and medium, the inhabitants of this new global village would, like those African villagers, demand ever greater involvement in the media that they spend their time with. Reading books, McLuhan believed, demanded all of our attention and allowed little time for our own participation in the medium, whereas the experience of watching television at home – the fuzzy, pulsating luminosity of the image and its relatively indistinct quality – allowed television viewers to involve themselves with the experience in a more formless, less analytical way. It was as if they had been hypnotised by it. By 1972, such was McLuhan's status as a celebrity intellectual that he was invited onto David Frost's television chatshow to explain his theories. In an attempt to illustrate the kind of involvement fostered by television, he threw out a striking comparison: the television viewer, McLuhan drily explained to David Frost and his worldwide television audience, tends to be so bombarded with images when watching television that they are left feeling 'stoned'. It was as if they were on a 'kind of inner trip'.

Television was but one small step in the direction of McLuhan's global village and was itself about to come under attack. In the late sixties and early seventies, as we saw in Chapter 3, some media activists and radical artists began to argue for cracking open the closed circuit of broadcast television to allow ordinary people into the loop. Only in the last decade, as millions of people spontaneously migrated to Cyburbia, was that idea fully realised. It had long shed its radical political undertone, but it was still deeply suspicious of its dealings with authority. Just as important, it was still flying the flag for an ethos of electronic activism. Most of what we do in Cyburbia, after all, demands that we remain actively engaged in its information loop at all times. The result, as we saw in Chapter 7, is that the traditional couch potato is in danger of becoming an endangered species. One good reason for our relentless activism in Cyburbia is that without it our homes in the place would quickly be overrun. When we are moved to fire off a stream of status updates to social networking devices like Facebook or Twitter to tell our electronic ties where we are or what we are doing ('James is writing a book at home'), we do so partly to keep the network and our status within it alive. Bloggers who stop updating their weblogs for a few days often return to find that their traffic has gone elsewhere, never to return. This new kind of involvement that we have with our electronic media, as we have seen, is much more intense and more pressing than anything Marshall McLuhan could have imagined. If watching TV was the media equivalent of being stoned, life in Cyburbia often seems like its crack cocaine.

Out of respect for its radical ancestry, let's call this new kind of electronic activism interactivism. Some date the birth of interactivism to the sudden appearance of the television remote control in the early eighties. For most of its short life the remote control has been incapable of allowing us any more freedom of movement than the ability to switch TV channels to something more interesting. Far more important was the fact that many of grew up hitched to the electronic information loop afforded us by computer games, mobiles and the internet. What that taught us, we saw in Chapter 6, was to respond rapidly to a continuous stream of electronic information. When we hop through TV channels using our remote it is because we are bored, but when we navigate a path through electronic information it is usually because we are intrigued enough to continue following our nose. To play an active part in an electronic information loop means not only following our nose but batting back feedback of our own too. Remember that Norbert Wiener envisaged the perfect social system as one knitted together by electronic information loops, each of which would be capable of feeding back information about the working of the system to ensure its smooth operation. As people took to spending more of their time on an electronic information loop, fringe theatre directors weren't the only ones to think about channelling this thirst for greater involvement in our media. Confronted with this riot of interactivism pushing at their doors, organisations of all kinds began to think about turning it to their own advantage.

Let's start with the time that we still spend watching the television. No one can fail to have noticed that TV programmes in which viewers are invited to vote via their mobile phone or their remote control – shows like *American Idol* in the United States, *Strictly Come Dancing* in the UK or *Torvill and Dean's Dancing on Ice* in Australia – now enjoy an avid following of millions. Since viewers are usually charged money in order to text in their vote, shows like this can be highly lucrative for the television companies that make them.

They can also, however, go horribly wrong. Late in 2007 a twenty-foot tall pink mechanical pig stuffed with pound coins and called the Jiggy Bank became the focus of a national scandal in Britain. Each week, in the company of two boyish light entertainers on a show called *Ant and Dec's Saturday Night Takeaway*, the Jiggy Bank was wheeled out to different locations where the winner of a text vote competition was required to ride it, rodeo-style, in the hope of dislodging some of those pound coins. The winners were not the only ones being taken for a ride. The Jiggy Bank was indeed ferried around the place, but twenty feet of plastic pig weighed down with pound coins was never going to get very far, and so the television researchers duly arrived at a short-list of potential viewers who happened to be close by. They also visited the homes of those on the shortlist to assess their likely reaction to winning, and how they might perform on the pig.

The Jiggy Bank was not the only one in the dock. The year 2007 was a disastrous one for executives working in British television as a succession of fakery scandals attracted record fines from the industry regulator and almost succeeded in bringing the entire industry to its knees. ITV stood accused of fleecing its audiences of money and systematically ignoring votes in interactive competitions. Most of those problems arose because previously passive coach potatoes were fast becoming active participants in the information loop. One investigation into irregularities in the set-up of various of those shows by a firm of accountants laid most of the blame at the door of the producers for exercising 'editorial judgement' over the registered preferences of electronic voters. 'Whilst this appears to have been done with the aim of producing the most entertaining programmes possible,' the accountants mused, 'clearly the exercise of editorial discretion in this way is fundamentally incompatible with fair conduct of viewer competitions or voting.' On *Soapstar Superstar*, a phone-in show that fell within the remit of the accountants, the producers were found to have simply ignored the viewers choice of which soap star should be invited to sing which songs and substituted their own selection instead.

This wasn't the first time that this kind of skulduggery had precipitated a collective beating of breasts within the TV industry. Exactly half a century earlier, a Columbia University professor called Charles Van Doren was making regular appearances as a contestant on *Twenty One*, a quiz show on American television. *Twenty One* had been dominated by an apparently unbeatable contestant called Herb Stempel, and its ratings were in the doldrums. As soon as the suave and apparently omniscient Van Doren arrived and toppled Stempel its audience figures shot up overnight. As the professor kept winning, he became a national celebrity and the name Van Doren a byword for braininess of the highest calibre. Van Doren, however, was not quite as brainy as he was made out to be. Not only had he been passed the answers in advance, but the producers had even coached him on how to wring the greatest possible drama from his performance at handing them over. When the scandal eventually broke in 1959, so heated was the hullabaloo that he ended up having to confess his deception to the less flattering glare of a House of Representatives investigation.

Watching all this from his base in Toronto, Marshall McLuhan could not see what all the fuss was about. 'Movies, in a sense, are also rigged shows,' he wrote in his book, *Understanding Media*. 'Any play or poem or novel is, also, rigged to produce an effect. So was the TV quiz show.' It was only our greater sense of involvement in the medium of television that had caused the outcry. Beneath his blithe apologetics for media's hall of mirrors, McLuhan's argument is just as relevant to the interactive entertainment which is now increasingly on offer on our TV screens. Viewers tune in to be entertained, to see something worth watching. On the other hand, their experience growing up on an electronic information loop has taught them to demand involvement with the medium. Television producers and editors, as a consequence, are increasingly asked to walk a tightrope between satisfying the demand for involvement and putting on an entertaining show. Faced with a piece of television that is in danger of unravelling before their eyes, it should come as no surprise that many of them quietly exercise their own judgement.

They aren't the only ones. On 23 January 2008 a lowly football team called Ebbsfleet United announced that it had sold itself to a consortium of twenty thousand fans who, grouped together in a website called MyFootballClub, would hence-forth have the power to pick the team. MyFootballClub took its cue from a fashionable idea known as crowdsourcing, which suggested that companies and organisations of all kinds could harness the wisdom of many different people via the internet rather than relying on the expertise of only a few pointy heads at the top. Given that crowds of football supporters are well known to have deeply felt opinions and imaginative ways of expressing them, professional football was thought to be an ideal way of turning the theory of crowdsourcing into practice. From here on in, Ebbsfleet fans were promised, they wouldn't need to shout insults at the manager after a bad result: from now on they *were* the manager.

The idea of passing control of a professional football club to a consortium of online enthusiasts was an audacious one. It was accepted in good spirit by Liam Daish, the former Republic of Ireland player who had the misfortune to be Ebbsfleet's manager before, under the new arrangements, he was rele-gated to head coach. He had good reason to keep his counsel. The club was deeply in debt and the cash stumped up by MyFootballClub – each of its members had coughed up an annual subscription of thirty-five pounds, giving the team a windfall of seven hundred thousand pounds – had effectively secured his wage packet. In interviews, however, Daish couldn't help but sound a little concerned at the new arrangements. 'My missus started asking me about formations and "who are you playing up front?"' he told one journalist. 'She's paid the thirty-five pounds and thinks I'm answerable to her now.' Behind the scenes, Daish was evidently hoping for a quiet life. 'I get the feeling,' he told another reporter, 'that a majority of people on MyFootballClub won't want to pick sides as they won't feel

qualified to do so.' He wasn't the only sceptic. Many of
Ebbsfleet's traditional supporters were aghast at the arrival of
this new electronic crowd, especially since they were drawn
from eighty countries around the world rather than native to
Kent. One supporters' club labelled the buyout as nothing
more than 'an extension of fantasy football'. Despite this, the
arrangement soon seemed to be working. Over the following
three months, Ebbsfleet lost only two of its ten games. Even
better, at the end of March the team managed to win its first-
ever place in the coveted 2008 FA Trophy Final at Wembley.
Members of MyFootballClub were granted the right to decide
ticket prices and which kit to buy – they voted, for example,
that the contract for producing their football strips should be
awarded to Nike. In theory they were also empowered to select
the team on a one-member, one-vote basis via the website. In
practise, however, nothing much happened. The first three
months of an 'acclimatisation period' in which the electronic
owners agreed not to interfere too much in choosing the team
came and went, but even after that the electronic fans still
hadn't got around to picking the team. As the big game
approached they eventually caved in and voted to let Liam
Daish have the final say on selecting the team. On 10 May
2008, after a dramatic 1–0 victory over Torquay United,
Ebbsfleet won the FA Trophy for the first time in its sixty-two-
year history. The team was doing very nicely indeed, but its
electronic fans had baulked at exercising their rights as its collective manager. Just as Liam Daish had predicted, they simply
weren't up to the job.

Tapping the electronic wisdom of crowds was only one way in
which those in authority were moving to take advantage of

interactivism, and it was one of the most primitive. Strictly speaking, it required that the judgements of each individual viewer, fan or contributor should be arrived at independently and then totted up at the end. In the language of quiz shows, there was to be no conferring.

In Cyburbia, however, with its constantly shifting conversation among a global community of peers, conferring is part of the point. Since this new kind of feedback travelled from peer to peer almost immediately, it could make massive electronic movements appear almost overnight. The muscle for these movements was often provided by armies of bloggers who, gifted with the ability to publish instantaneously and banded together in continuous conversation with their online peers, began to pursue an asymmetrical, sniping war against the established media, picking off examples of disinformation and subjecting vested insider interests to vigorous and relentless attack. These bedroom-bunkered *pyjamadeen* liked to see themselves as outsiders battling against hostile and entrenched elites. Whether their barbs were aimed from the political right or left, their modus operandi – their sometimes paranoid distrust of authority, their enthusiasm for raising consciousness among like-minded peers and their relentless partisanship over cool-headed objective analysis – looked like an electronic echo of what had once been called the counter-culture.

For some, being talked about in Cyburbia could be very good news. Beginning in the year 2005 Tony Bilsborough, a marketer at the British chocolate maker Cadbury, became aware of internet chatter demanding the rehabilitation of a defunct chocolate bar called the Wispa. The bar, launched in 1981 as a firmer and more velvety alternative to the bubble-filled Aero, had initially enjoyed a good run, but by the close of the nineties sales had plummeted and Cadbury finally made the decision to put it out of its misery in 2003. The company had, however, failed to appreciate the growing popularity of the Wispa as an emblem as a certain kind of eighties kitsch. By the summer of 2007, according to Bilsborough, there were over a hundred 'Bring Back Wispa' campaigns – with nearly fourteen thousand members – on blogs and social networking sites. Petitions aimed at Cadbury ricocheted their way around the internet as people forwarded them on to their peers. A film was posted on YouTube, urging people to bring their influence to bear on the company. In August 2007 the campaign spilled over into real life when several pro-Wispa activists stormed the stage at Glastonbury during a performance by Iggy Pop to unfurl a 'Bring Back Wispa' banner. A few weeks later both Bilsborough and Cadbury succumbed and agreed to resurrect the bar. In doing nothing but listening out for feedback and then acting on it, Cadbury had scored a huge publicity coup and won a devoted body of fans for its aerated chocolate bar. In fact, doing nothing was one of the reasons why it worked so well. Tony Bilsborough knew enough about social networking sites to know that it was not his party – and that if he tried to crash it both he and Cadbury would likely fall flat on their faces. His only contact with the Wispa activists was to post them a few free boxes of Wispas once their efforts had been successful. It was hard to find their addresses, because he didn't even know who they were.

As more and more people migrated to blogs, chatrooms and online social networks in Cyburbia, marketers couldn't resist joining them there and, under cover of the internet, deliberately trying to foment the kind of electronic 'buzz' that had spontaneously erupted around the Wispa. Since people go to

Cyburbia in search of an intimate and authentic channel for communication, they make for a highly impressionable audience. One popular technique was to 'seed' something which looked authentic and hip enough to go 'viral' – to be passed around from peer to peer in a kind of human network effect. In December 2006 passers-by in Cyburbia noticed the appearance of an odd-looking website in which two teenage boys told of their enthusiasm for Sony's latest gaming console, the PSP, and how much they wanted one for Christmas. In an accompanying video on YouTube, the pair could be seen going through the motions of jigging around to the following rap:

I love the big screen
So fresh and so clean
It's all in my dreams
And makes me want to scream
Games so crazy
They totally amaze me.

This excruciating exercise in deliberate fakery was, as it took about half an hour for internet users to decipher, the work of none other than Sony itself. Under pressure from its rival Nintendo, the company had employed a marketing agency called Zipatoni to orchestrate the whole operation. Zipatoni specialised in zany campaigns; so zany were its operatives that they used their business address to buy the internet domain name they had bought for the job, enabling online gamers to rumble them almost instantly. The torrent of invective that followed was so merciless that it demolished any credibility the company had with its teenage market. 'For the love of God,' one former PSP fan wrote in an angry open letter to Sony on an internet bulletin board, 'stop treating us like idiots; we can make or break a company so treat us with some fucking respect.' An intervention that, unlike the efforts of Sony's rappers, didn't even rhyme.

Such crude attempts to manufacture buzz were easily swatted away by the hordes of young people who watch over the web. Sony's marketers had fallen foul of Cyburbia's equivalent of a neighbourhood watch and were swiftly apprehended. It didn't stop others from trying. The year before Sony's marketing disaster, McDonald's had tried to cook up some controversy by paying a couple to blog excitedly about their discovery that one of their McDonald's French fries was the spitting image of Abraham Lincoln. The French fry in question, it transpired, was actually ten centimetres long and made out of plastic. To the sniggers of just about everyone on the internet, it looked nothing like Lincoln, and not much like a French fry either.

What tripped up Sony's fake rappers and McDonald's curiously shaped French fry was a kind of information feedback loop, but not the sort they had been hoping for. The flood of abuse was very similar to the 'bad' or destructive feedback that, as we saw in Chapter 3, was threatened by new media activists in the late sixties if their demands for greater involvement in mainstream media were ignored or patronised. What they had plotted was to deliberately feed back into the loop information which tended to disrupt the system rather than make it run more smoothly. A simple version of this kind of destructive feedback can be seen in the quarrels that now regularly break out between audiences and programme-makers over interactive game shows. When the rock singer Chris Daughtry was dismissed from *American Idol* in May 2006 his

fans were so incensed that they set about organising loud petitions demanding a recount and spreading unsubstantiated
allegations that the vote had been rigged. Petitions and slan-
der, however, are the only way in which audiences can get
their own back. On some shows the professional judges hired
to pontificate in television studios began to suspect that electronic voters were deliberately frustrating their efforts by
giving their favourite performers the thumbs-down. In
September 2007, following complaints by the judges on
Strictly Come Dancing that their favourite dancers were systematically being given the heave-ho by the mischievous voters
at home, the BBC abruptly changed the voting format to let the
judges have the final say.

With the steady population of Cyburbia by millions of
online peers, that information feedback loop between audience
and institution was given an enormous fillip. Whereas previously internet users could only communicate directly with
authority – and often find that their responses were filed in an
electronic wastebasket – now they could join a conversation of
millions feeding information back and forth about the machi-
nations of those in authority and their dealings with them.
Faced with this onslaught of information as feedback, many
mainstream media outlets saw an opportunity to invite the
inhabitants of Cyburbia into their information loop in order to
improve the efficiency of their operation. It was, however,
easier said than done. When information was solicited from
online peers and then rigorously checked by those in charge,
electronic crowds could work impressively quickly to correct
errors and tap new sources of information. But make the mistake of promising more profound involvement and the results
were usually ruinous. Take an experiment mounted by the

publishing company Penguin UK when it invited millions of web users to collaborate on a 'group novel' called *A Million Penguins*. Over six weeks, beginning on 1 February 2007, a blank page was pushed out onto the web to be written on by anonymous online scribes. In keeping with the collaborative spirit of the enterprise anyone was allowed to add, edit or delete what had gone before. *A Million Penguins* was swiftly hailed as a 'global experiment in new media writing'. Such was its ambition that it even borrowed its opening line from *Jane Eyre*. 'There was no possibility of taking a walk that day,' it began, before beginning its inevitable hurtle downhill. Characters multiplied out of control, paragraphs and whole sections ended at random, plotlines drifted hopelessly and were left hanging in mid-air. The story was so chaotic as to be unreadable, and was constantly splintering off in new directions; at one point it even divided itself into 'Novel A' and 'Novel B', with links to alternative endings. Some collaborative novelists took it upon themselves to try to sabotage the whole experiment; one took the trouble to litter the text with references to bananas. In the end the organisers were forced to 'lock down' the project for a few hours every day in order to ward off the vandals and purge the novel of its accumulation of spam and non-sequiturs. Over the course of its short life, fifteen hundred people had participated in the writing of *A Million Penguins*; together they had made a total of eleven thousand edits. Putting a brave face on the alphabet soup that resulted from all this activity, the editor responsible for the project, Jon Elek, noted that his book was 'not the most read, but certainly the most written novel in history'. That was putting it mildly. It became apparent that one of the reasons for the novel's incoherence was that not even the masses of novelists who had queued up to help write the book had bothered to read what had gone before. They were too busy writing.

One way of looking at the vandalism inflicted on *A Million Penguins* was as a kind of two-fingered feedback on the silliness of the whole idea in the first place. Publishers were not its only victims. When the *Los Angeles Times* had the idea of allowing its readers to rewrite each day's editorial online in June 2005 readers responded by flooding the site with porn photos and foul language. Three days later came the inevitable editorial tombstone. 'Unfortunately,' it conceded, 'we have had to remove this feature, at least temporarily, because a few readers were flooding the site with inappropriate material.' The *LA Times* experiment, just like Penguin's failed attempt to persuade an electronic crowd to co-write a novel, pointed to a deeper problem with inviting electronic activists into the workings of professional media. Throwing open one's organisation to electronic feedback worked only until its beneficiaries realise that, no matter how many messages they fire off, those in authority are ultimately bound to retain the reins of editorial control. At that point it is highly likely that they will switch from offering 'good' or helpful feedback to pushing 'bad' or destructive feedback back into the system. The angry, splenetic or downright offensive tone sometimes exhibited by bloggers is a good example of this kind of feedback. Frustrated at their lack of control over professional media, bloggers are often tempted to get together to post angry or abusive messages on the outlets of those they don't like – so-called 'flaming'. The effect is similar to an annoying screech or howl, akin to the noise which occurs when output from a sound system finds its way back into the input.

Feedback from Cyburbia doesn't need to be deliberately destructive to lob a spanner into the information works. Just as bloggers need to update their weblogs constantly and people who fire off e-mails often remark at how tricky it can be to close an exchange of communication, journalists who enter into electronic conversations with their readers often report that it becomes difficult to close that information loop and pull away to get some work done. As newspapers and other media outlets move their material online, too, they can't help but pay more attention to statistics on how many people click on particular stories; many even feature on their front page a rolling list of which stories are proving the most popular. An up-to-the-minute list of what one's electronic peers are clicking on makes intriguing reading, and will undoubtedly inspire many readers to click on some of those stories themselves. As we saw in Chapter 5, collective judgements about quality tend to get snagged in an instantly self-reinforcing feedback loop whereby things become more and more successful simply because they were favoured by those who happened to arrive earlier. If data on the popularity of news stories were to further feed back into judgements about which kinds of stories should be covered, newsrooms would end up chasing their own tails – and abandoning their judgement to the random whims and enthusiasms of Cyburbia.

It isn't only electronic conversations with readers and electronic popularity contests that can sometimes feed back into the decision-making loop of professional journalists. Just as we saw in Chapter 5 that inhabitants of Cyburbia need to 'tag' themselves and their profiles with keywords so that they can be picked up by their peers on search engines, anecdotal evidence suggests that some journalists writing for online editions are being encouraged to seed their stories with keywords that happen to be popular among those who are typing them into Google. If this were to become commonplace, it would bring the global electronic network promised by the gurus of cybernetics to a terrifying denouement. At the wrong end of a sophisticated electronic information loop tying them to the inchoate impulses and musings of millions of internet users, journalists would find themselves strapped uncomfortably into our electronic id – and feeding it back to us in the reports that they produce.

Organisations that invite traffic from Cyburbia through their front gate often get more than they bargained for. There is no doubt that Cyburbia's burgeoning neighbourhood watch, if it can be put to work, makes for a great new way to correct errors and rope in new sources of information. Go further and invite these electronic crowds into your own decision-making loop, however, and the results often look more like a wrecking ball.

None of this should be at all surprising. Electronic activism of the kind that has grown to populate Cyburbia, as we have seen, is deeply hostile to any kind of authority. For organisations, the bigger problem with opening up their decision-making loop to feedback from Cyburbia was that they might end up surrendering their judgement to an electronic crowd. If the idea of throwing open the door to electronic feedback was to quicken the pace of organisational decision-making and free people up to take the initiative, that's not what happened. Just as switching between too many streams of electronic information while we work can often slow us down, paying too much attention to a constant stream of electronic instructions can often end up blunting or befuddling the judgement of those in charge. In paying too much heed to the traffic in Cyburbia, the danger is that they end up paralysed and unable to make effective decisions of their own.

Given the problems that arise when electronic feedback is handed a degree of control, whatever are those in charge to do with it? Perhaps the most important lesson is to realise that unless those in authority steer oncoming electronic traffic it will end up steering itself and taking them with it. Think again about the confusion that overcame those who attended that unconventional production of *The Masque of the Red Death*. As members of the audience they revelled in the fact that they were actively participating in the performance. To some extent they were, but they were also being ushered around the building with great precision. Like the anti-aircraft gunner upon whom Norbert Wiener based his theory of cybernetics and those film and TV directors we encountered in Chapter 6, the director of *The Masque of the Red Death* allowed his audience to zigzag around to their hearts' content, safe in the knowledge that he was so far ahead of them he would always have them covered. In doing so he satisfied the thirst of his audience for greater involvement without surrendering any control of his work. Like a matador he let them follow their own nose and charge this way and that, but remained firmly in control of the show.

The need to steer electronic traffic rather than to be steered by it was a lesson that was always going to be lost on the most scrupulous disciples of cybernetics. Central to the whole idea was Wiener's hunch that laying an electronic information loop between humans could give rise to a system that was so self-steering it would appear to be automatic. From its origins in the military-industrial establishment, his cybernetic idea had conquered the counter-culture and the computer industry, and from its beachhead there it had grown to mould our cultural life and even our psyche. Its full mettle had remained in abeyance for decades while it awaited technological improvements and more widespread public interest, but with the steady population of Cyburbia it had now returned triumphant to face down the mainstream media. Its journey, however, was far from over. Media organisations, it turned out, weren't the only ones trying to thread an electronic information loop through their operations in an effort to make them steer themselves at the beginning of the twenty-first century. Strange new wars were breaking out and military strategists were searching for new ideas with which to fight them. Cybernetics was on its way back home.

9

Network Failure

During the summer of 2002, in an incident which military officials did their best to cover up, an evil Middle Eastern dictator inflicted one of the most humiliating defeats on the US armed forces that it has ever known. The bulk of a large and well-protected American Expeditionary Force, sixteen ships along with the aircraft carrier at the head of the fleet, was bombed to smithereens and their remains sent straight to the bottom of the Persian Gulf. When all the casualties and damage was totted up, it was the worst naval disaster since Pearl Harbor.

Except that it wasn't real. It was all a game, and the evil dictator was played by a sixty-four-year-old Vietnam veteran and lifelong Republican voter called Paul K. Van Riper. Van Riper, a tall, square-jawed man with a distinctly military bearing, had been living in comfortable retirement since 1997, when he had left the Marines Corps as a Lieutenant General. To keep himself busy he had taken an occasional job as consultant to some of the wargame exercises that the Pentagon uses to punctuate its military calendar. He was a good choice. Van Riper was known to be one of the US Army's most imaginative military strategists, as well a fiercely independent thinker who loved nothing more than to poke fun at its military's top brass. The usual drill in Pentagon wargames is to pit a 'Blue' or American team against an enemy force known only as Red. Van Riper always seemed to get the job of playing the enemy; his maverick credentials must have helped, along with the fact that his friends liked to call him Rip. In the spring of 2000, Pentagon officials approached Rip and invited him to take part in what was going to be the biggest and most expensive war game ever seen. The whole thing, Van Riper was told, was going to be two years in the making, its codename was to be Millennium Challenge, its budget was to be 250 million dollars and its battle plan was to involve nearly fourteen thousand American soldiers, supported by planes and warships; to add to the scale of the confrontation, real battles were going to be buttressed with virtual simulations on powerful computers around the world. It came as no surprise to Van Riper that he was being invited to play Red.

Millennium Challenge, Van Riper knew very well when he accepted the job of Red commander, was designed to test out new military kit and ideas associated with something called the Revolution in Military Affairs (RMA). RMA was an acronym that had hung around for about a decade in military think-tanks and was now finally being taken seriously, mainly because the incoming Defense Secretary, Donald Rumsfeld, had long been a fan. Rumsfeld had spent much of the previous two decades in exile from government working as a business executive, where he had seen what information networks could do.

As soon as he was appointed to the post of Defense Secretary in January 2001 he announced his intention to transform the American military in the image of the RMA – to update its sluggish cold-war military machine to take advantage of the same information technology that had done so much to power the American economy. In a famous speech delivered on 10 September 2001, Rumsfeld railed against a military machine that was 'one of the last bastions of central planning' and which needed to be taken by the scruff of the neck if it was to adapt to the more agile, information-based force needed to protect America in the twenty-first century.

High on the intellectual agenda of those in favour of the military transformation was another cumbersome acronym, NCW – network-centric warfare. The idea of NCW had been touted since the middle of the nineties and, like RMA, was modelled on the way in which information networks had become vitally important to the American economy at around the same time. NCW was first floated in a military report commissioned by the US Department of Defense in 1996. Its champions argued that the old way of fighting wars – in which massive, hierarchically organised armies were arraigned to fight each other to the death on huge battlefields – was coming to a close. In future, they said, war was more likely to be waged in cities than on battlefields and would likely be fought against small groups of nimble guerrilla fighters than well-dug-in national armies. In these new kinds of wars, access to high-tech information would be crucial because it would enable those who had their fingers on the trigger to respond rapidly and decisively. Information sensors on the ground and in the air would be linked to command centres and from there directly to soldiers; spy drones flying directly

overhead would provide instant information about the status of
the enemy. The idea was to tighten as much as possible the
information loop 'between sensor and shooter' so as to allow
soldiers on the ground to move with maximum speed and
agility. The idea, rooted in cybernetic principles, was that
tying together all the different nodes in the military's network in a single information loop would give troops the
clearest possible picture of the battlefield, allowing everyone to
act in concert and making the enemy's communications seem
primitive in comparison. The plan was nothing less than to
eliminate the 'fog of war' and replace it with 'complete situational awareness' – to make sure everyone knew what everyone
else was doing and what was going on all of the time.

The slow march of RMA and NCW divided the American
armed forces. One the one hand, military leaders wanted all the
technological kit that they could get and were well aware that
technology is often the trump card that can make the difference between victory and defeat. On the other, they hated the
gobbledegook that often came with it and worried that, amid
all this fancy jargon about military transformation, expensive
new communication gizmos were going to end up taking the
place of boots on the ground. Paul Van Riper wasn't at all
hostile to the use of new high-tech weaponry or communications. The American public just needed to be sure, he felt, that
the technology it was buying served a definite purpose, serving
military objectives rather than the other way around. 'Bytes of
information,' Rip was fond of saying, 'can be very valuable in
war, but it's bullets that kill enemies.' Terms such as 'information dominance' and 'network-centric warfare', he reckoned,
were inclined to make the business of war look machine-like
and antiseptic. 'They don't understand that it's a terrible,

uncertain, chaotic, bloody business.' As a Vietnam vet, Van Riper was haunted by the way that engineering and systems theory, allied to number-crunching computers, had been used by the then Defense Secretary, Robert McNamara, to argue that America's war in Vietnam was winnable, even when the soldiers on the ground knew that it wasn't. Despite the reservations of many military commanders, RMA and NCW were slowly becoming the holy grail of military planning and acquisition and, by the time Millennium Challenge came around in 2002, it was clear that it was supposed to rubber-stamp those new doctrines that now had backing from the very top. 'Experiments like Millennium Challenge,' said Donald Rumsfeld at the time, 'are very important to future battlefield successes. It will help us to create a force that is not only interoperable, responsive, agile and lethal, but also one that is capable of capitalising on the information revolution and the advancements in technology that are available today.' According to the wordy official executive report on the wargame issued after it was played by the United States Joint Forces Command (JFCOM), 'it describes a way to defeat a complex, adaptive enemy by understanding his capabilities in terms of his political, military, economic, social, infrastructure and information systems; identifying key nodes and links in those systems; and then attacking the coherence of those systems – reducing the whole to less than the sum of its parts.'

That wasn't, however, what happened at all. In JFCOM's entire twenty-two-page report on how Millennium Challenge had played out, the only clue that things hadn't gone as planned was a reference to 'a renegade element within the Red leadership [that] conducted broad actions, including conventional military, asymmetric, diplomatic, information, economic, and terrorist applications, with the goal of establishing regional power and control'. That was wrapping it up in jargon, and putting it rather mildly. As part of his Red force, it turned out, Van Riper had been given a computer-generated flotilla of small boats, which he kept buzzing around what was supposed to be the Persian Gulf. As the Blue fleet of US Navy warships and Marine amphibious vessels sailed into the Persian Gulf they assumed that their superior technology and communications would win out, so Blue's commander sent a message ordering Red to surrender or face annihilation. Unbeknownst to the Blue team, however, Van Riper had packed his small patrol boats and small propeller aircraft with explosives. Upon Rip giving the order, those apparently harmless boats suddenly converged to become lethal, ramming their way into Blue boats and aircraft carriers in orchestrated suicide attacks. On a roll, Rip then fired off a few cruise missiles from one of his small boats and sank Blue's only aircraft carrier. For good measure, he even set about contaminating one of Blue's airfields with chemical weapons.

It was at this point that military referees arrived to tell Rip that enough was enough. They wanted to restart the whole exercise and so Blue team's fleet was duly re-floated and Van Riper's Red team put back in its corner. Once again, however, Rip came out punching below the belt. This time he was informed that he wasn't allowed to use his expensive microwave communication systems, and was also told to turn a blind eye to Blue's aerial manoeuvres. It wasn't as bad as all that – he could, they reminded him, still use satellites and mobile phones to talk to his troops and keep tabs on the battlefield. Rip still refused to play ball. He and his Red team took to using motorcycle messengers to convey instructions, and to making coded announcements to his team from the minarets of mosques during calls to prayer, thereby ducking under the high-tech eavesdropping and jamming capabilities of Blue. In total the game was restarted three times, until Van Riper became aware that his subordinates were being leaned on by the game's administrators to ignore his commands, and quit in disgust. In a long e-mail to the organisers of the wargame at JFCOM, he complained that the referees of the competition had tried to give Blue a leg-up again and again without taking on board the lessons of his unconventional approach. 'It simply became a scripted exercise,' Van Riper said, and one whose only purpose was to validate the concepts and the high-tech communications equipment that cheerleaders for RMA and NCW were desperate to buy into. Just as the technology boosters had overplayed their hand in the late nineties when they claimed that the internet could overthrow the laws of economics, supporters of the Revolution in Military Affairs made the mistake of thinking that their high-tech military kit could on its own rewrite the basic rules of how to wage war. In fact, until the news of Van Riper's daring acts of sabotage were exposed by a journalist from the *New York Times*, the whole thing was being trumpeted as a success for the new military doctrines. The American military was preparing for information-based war, and too much was at stake to allow Paul Van Riper to blow it out of the water.

The irony in the Pentagon's attempt to jump-start its forces into the information age was almost heartening. Cybernetic ideas about the importance of information loops, which had their roots in the battle to shoot down German bombers during the

Second World War, were now, after a lengthy sojourn as consultants to business transformation, being pressed back into military service to fight a very different kind of enemy. Cybernetics took an unusual route into American military culture. Norbert Wiener's idea of cybernetic man, in which humans were hitched to and animated by a continuous electronic information loop of instructions and feedback, had started out as no more than a suggestive metaphor to help military engineers build better systems for shooting down enemy aircraft. Passed through the hands of electro-hippies, it was also an inspiration to those who patched together early prototypes of the internet. But if cybernetics was to convince ordinary soldiers as well as boffins and electro-hippies, it would need to find a bona fide military man prepared to vouch for its potential on the battlefield.

In a former fighter pilot called John Boyd it found the perfect candidate. John Boyd's contribution to military cybernetics can be dated to 4 April 1965. On that day four US Air Force F-105 Thunderchief fighter-bombers – known to those who flew them as 'Thuds' – set out on a top secret bombing raid on North Vietnam. Out of nowhere a gang of Russian-made MiG-17 fighter planes lunged into their airspace and, before any of them could react, two of the American fighters were shot down. A third, damaged but still flying, made off in an attempt to get back to base. The pilot of the fourth American plane, attempting to give some cover to the third, discovered that one of the MiG-17s had somehow managed to get behind him and put him in the line of fire. Each time the Thud pilot moved the MiG was able to cut corners and manoeuvre more quickly to put him back in range. Running out of gambits, the American pilot remembered a briefing given to him by the instructor, John Boyd, on his combat training programme back in Nevada. If you ever end up with a MiG on your tail and were out of options, he remembered Boyd telling him, the only thing to do was to perform a 'snap-roll' – to suddenly slam on the brakes and turn the plane violently to its side so that it corkscrewed around the horizontal axis while maintaining the same approximate direction. In a plane like the F-105, such a manoeuvre would slow movement so abruptly that it would emerge from its loop behind its opponent rather than in front. Sure enough, when the pilot did as his instructor suggested, his plane decelerated so sharply that the MiG was forced out in front. The unusual move was so bizarre that it managed to disorient both parties. The American pilot was so bewildered by his success that he even forgot to pull the trigger, and both pilots went back to their bases alive.

Colonel John Boyd's military career had begun in the early fifties, when he had persuaded his Air Force superiors to let him fly fighter planes in Korea. No sooner had he got there than he became obsessed with the minutiae of air-to-air combat strategy. A fast talker and a frenetically restless mind, such was the spew of food and spittle from his mouth when he held forth on his favourite subject in the military canteen that some of his colleagues began to complain about his table manners. To help shut him up, his colleagues eventually made Boyd the tactical instructor for the entire squadron. In that role, one of his favourite routines was to make all new trainee air pilots aware of a standing bet. He would allow any of them to start an engagement on his tail, and wager that within just forty seconds he could beat any of them in air-to-air combat or he would hand over forty dollars to his challenger. Sure enough, once in the air Boyd would suddenly perform his trademark snap-roll and throw the trainee out in front and into his sights. The unorthodox manoeuvre was dangerous and heretical to those in high command, but 'Forty-Second Boyd' was never known to have lost money.

By the sixties, John Boyd's tactical briefings were playing to packed seminar rooms, and he was invited to help the US Air Force design the next generation of American fighter planes. Reading up on his brief, it wasn't long before he began to notice something odd. In Korea, Boyd remembered, despite flying planes that were slower than their rivals he and his fellow fighter pilots were shooting down ten times as many planes as the Koreans. In the war in Vietnam, however, there had been a definite falling-off in the performance of American air-fighters despite their increased speed. His suspicions were redoubled after the disappointing performance of the Thuds in North Vietnam; the F-105 fighter-bomber, after all, was one of the US Air Force's newest planes and twice as fast as the MiGs that it was up against. When news of the incident filtered back to military high command it was Boyd who was summoned to the Pentagon and asked to explain what could be done. His answer was forthright: the new Russian-made MiGs might be slower than the F-105, but they had much better manoeuvrability in the air, and much better systems for perceiving where they were and where their enemies were. Since the war in Korea American military designers had been obsessed with making their planes go faster, but Boyd was able to tell them that absolute speed was often less important than situational awareness – the ability to find your enemy before he found you, and the ability to change rapidly from one state to another so as to confuse him and wriggle out of his

sights. It wasn't so much speed which proved crucial in air-to-
air dogfights but agility – the ability to zigzag around in
response to new information.

This was the epiphany that was to shape the rest of John
Boyd's career. In the years that followed, Boyd thought
through its implications and boiled them down to a simple
series of manoeuvres that, he believed, could help steal the
march in just about any competitive endeavour. Faced with an
intractable enemy buzzing around you, Boyd liked to lecture
his trainee fighter pilots, the first thing to do was to observe
your opponent – to see him before he sees you. Then you need
to orient yourself to that information, to try to make sense of
it by putting it in some kind of context. Having accomplished
both of those, you need to decide what to do next. Lastly, you
must act on that decision before your enemy can shoot you out
of the sky. Boyd dubbed this constant and continuous cycle of
observe-orient-decide-act the OODA loop and, according to
him, anyone who cycled through this decision-making loop
faster than his opponent would likely emerge victorious. By
making one's OODA loop shorter and more fluid than one's
opponent's, Boyd reasoned, the fighter pilot would not only
have a greater chance of getting in the first shot; by zigzagging
around in instantaneous response to new information he could
also sow confusion in his adversary, thereby lengthening his
information loop and knocking him off balance. As Boyd put
it in pep-talks to the trainees under his wing, 'He who can
handle the quickest rate of change survives.'

Over the following decades, John Boyd's OODA loop evolved
into a doctrine of almost metaphysical depth and Boyd himself
became a military legend. Its influence extended far beyond the
US Air Force: in 1989 the US Marines incorporated it into their

war fighting manual. The OODA loop certainly made for a useful rule of thumb for how to react in combat conditions so as to outfox the enemy. As it was interpreted by military commanders, however, its only moral was to favour the rapid processing of electronic information and the rapid reaction to that information. The first lesson of the OODA loop was the vital importance of being plugged into a continuous electronic information loop like that enjoyed by a fighter pilot. Its second was an imperative to act on that information, and a warning against getting stuck in an indecisive cycle of observation and orientation – what some dubbed an 'OO-OO-OO-OO' loop. 'Intellectuals pride themselves with their OOOOing,' noted one hard-nosed military disciple of Boyd, with a hint of campness, 'but they accomplish nothing of substance.'

John Boyd's OODA loop bore a remarkable similarity to the cybernetic information loop envisaged by Norbert Wiener. It seemed an uncanny coincidence, too, that both of them had uncovered very similar general theories of human behaviour while patiently observing the movement of military aircraft and how best to shoot them down. As an obsessive reader of cybernetics and systems theory, Boyd would certainly have come across Wiener's work. Both he and Wiener found inspiration in engineering theory, and both explained the relationship between individuals and their environment in terms of a boundless series of information feedback loops. In their own ways both brought to war-making the idea that military operations and equipment should be seen as a single, living information system rather than a series of war machines that could be divided back into the sum of their parts. It was the former fighter pilot rather than the mathematician-intellectual, however, who succeeded in establishing cybernetics into the culture of the American military.

Supporters of the idea of network-centric warfare and information-based war were impressed by Boyd's idea that military operations could be seen as systems animated by a continuous flow of information around them, and inspired by his suggestion that one could act to use that information to react rapidly and throw the enemy off guard. In the aftermath of the terrorist attacks of 11 September 2001, for example, generals and military-minded politicians all queued up to praise Boyd's ideas. A year after that, when the JFCOM briefing the Millennium Challenge wargame announced that the next war 'is not just going to be military on military . . . the decisive factor is how you take apart your adversary's system', it did so with more than a nod to the ideas of John Boyd.

Enthusiasts for the idea of network-centric warfare weren't the only ones who considered themselves indebted to John Boyd. Like Boyd, Paul Van Riper was a natural maverick who had little faith in military bureaucracy and groupthink; he even listed Boyd and his OODA loop as one of his chief influences as a military strategist. What's more, when Millennium Challenge was finally played it was JFCOM's high-tech communications system which was taken apart rather than the other way around, and precisely because Van Riper's Red team didn't rely too heavily on electronic communications and used their initiative instead. In contrast, the Blue team were distracted by all the electronic information at their fingertips and were convinced of their all-seeing omnipotence. The best way to disrupt the OODA loop of an enemy that has become too dependent on high-tech communications, Van Riper reasoned, was to resist its lure and play a radically different game. Get too caught up in the information loop, as he put it, 'and you drown in the data'.

By the time it came to play Millennium Challenge, of course, the American military was squaring up to mount an invasion of Iraq and it didn't take a military genius to work out who Paul Van Riper's Red team was supposed to stand for. Van Riper's immediate concern was that, amid all this fancy jargon about agility and adaptability, the Defense Department was building up to prosecute a war with too much unnecessary technology and too few men on the ground. At first, the three-week campaign of 'shock and awe' seemed to vindicate the doctrine of network-centric warfare. The invasion had succeeded in disabling much of Iraq's infrastructure and utilities, bringing the country to a halt while coalition soldiers advanced on Baghdad. New technology was rolled out to tighten up information loops 'between sensor and shooter' so that every node in the military network could be in constant communication with the others, and rapidly responsive to the information that came its way. For the soldiers on the ground, having all this communications equipment at their disposal must have seemed reassuring. Many of them would have grown up honing their skills by playing computer games and surfing the internet, and many more had been trained using army-sponsored 3D video simulations. Now they had at their disposal digital maps and global positioning systems capable of reading their location and that of everyone else on the battlefield. Unmanned predator drones, navigated by joystick-wielding air force pilots at an airbase thousands of miles away in Las Vegas, flew over Iraq and Afghanistan seeking out information about the location of insurgents to send back into their information loop. America's National Security Agency even established a giant online chatroom for US forces in Iraq; its codename was Zircon Chat and the idea was that it would fuse intelligence and military operations on the ground, enabling up to two thousand people to be connected, live and continuously, to the same information loop. Some of the younger troops seem to have taken to the new technology with great enthusiasm. Amid all these new communication gizmos there were plenty of opportunities for soldiers to chat amongst themselves about where they were and what they were up to – a kind of military equivalent of twittering or updating their profiles on Facebook. In their spare time some of them established peer-to-peer communications channels like Companycommand and Platoonleader, with which they could whisper tips about how to respond to insurgent attacks out of earshot of their commanders. Lively discussion threads emerged with different views on subjects such as how to lay sandbags on the floor of vehicles, or with admonitions to look up as well as to the sides while driving through built-up areas.

Within months of the invasion of Iraq occupation gave way to a vicious insurgency and the idea that wars could be won from the air and from space via satellites, sensors and precision weapons soon came unstuck. It also became clear that the US military had failed to learn from Millennium Challenge, that a high-tech information loop could be vulnerable to unconventional Iraqi guerrilla attacks and suicide bombings. By the end of March 2003 William Wallace, the commander of the US Army Forces in the Persian Gulf, was grumbling that 'the enemy we're fighting is a bit different than the one we war-gamed against'. The problem was that, in a battle against rag-tag armies of insurgents, overwhelming superiority in communications technology was of limited use and could prove a dangerous distraction. Despite all its promises it did nothing to eliminate the fog of war. For one thing, there are limits to how much raw data humans can absorb, particularly while staring at a screen in the middle of a battle. Just as we saw in Chapter 7, that switching constantly in and out of different tasks or connections can be counter-productive in the office, attempting to keep abreast of too many different streams of battlefield information could easily confuse troops and slow them down on the battlefield. In any case, much of the information received in the thick of conflict tended to be of doubtful value – and the more nodes in the information loop, the greater was the potential for confusion, contradiction and unnecessary chatter.

But that wasn't the only problem with the US military's high-tech interpretation of John Boyd's OODA loop. Not only was there a danger that those in the information loop would get bogged down in data – the 'OO' (Observe-Orient) of Boyd's cycle – but there was also a risk that their rapid reaction to that information might lead them into making hasty decisions – the 'DA' (Decide-Act). Tighten too far the information loop between electronic sensor and shooter and the danger was that soldiers would get jumpy and fire at the wrong targets. Further proof, if any was required, that the electronic information loop was not all that it promised to be arrived when, during a follow-up to Millennium Challenge in May 2004, the reliance by the US military on satellite imagery and airborne sensors played right into the enemy's hands. Just like Paul Van Riper, the enemy Red commander in this wargame chose guerrilla-style tactics and decided to overwhelm Blue's sensors by dispersing his forces throughout the country. Red succeeded in throwing up so much confusion that, even though Blue boasted very sophisticated technology, his information pipelines were soon overloaded and the Blue commanders had difficulty understanding what they were seeing on their screens.

Coalition forces in Iraq, moreover, were not the only organisation with access to an electronic information loop. Many of the insurgent groups had begun to use the internet as their primary means of communication. For small bands of guerrillas with little access to the mainstream media, the ability to burrow under the control of the authorities and post up their propaganda all over Cyburbia proved much more useful than it could ever be for a conventional army. Some e-mailed daily bulletins, while others took to bringing digital cameras with them on manoeuvres so that they could upload footage of their operations to the internet. Thanks to nimble new operators in the subterranean world of online media in Western countries who routinely monitor extremist jihadi websites, that footage immediately flew around the world. In April 2005, for example, watching a BBC News Online report on an incident in Iraq in which a helicopter had been shot from the sky and eleven security guards were killed, I noticed that the footage displayed the insignia of the insurgents themselves, the Islamic Army of Iraq. From the safety of my attic desk I Googled 'Islamic Army in Iraq' and very quickly discovered an expertly produced five-minute version of the incident on a Western website. The first thing the viewer sees is a shot of the aircraft being hit by a rocket-propelled grenade and careering to the ground. Then the charred wreckage appears, along with gruesome close-ups of the burned and dismembered bodies of the security contractors. And then something infinitely more horrible happens. As the cameraman and his comrade wander around filming the wreckage they see a slightly wounded survivor of the crash lying in long grass. As the man gets to his feet the cameraman appears to direct him to stand in a certain spot, as if he's a guest in a wedding video. On cue he is executed by a volley of rifle shots from other gunmen, and the film finishes with his executioners continuing to fire bullets into his dead body.

Most of us would rather not see such things, but many are taking a peek at them while no one else is about. The site on which I found the Islamic Army in Iraq video was a niche social networking site called Ogrish (it has since changed its name to LiveLeak), which started out inviting viewers to share their pictures of disasters such as car crashes and murders. During the war in Iraq it became a repository of bloody images from war zones that other media outlets found too tasteless to show. Since Ogrish hovers on the fringes of legality in many European countries, its staff are necessarily cagey about their operations. When I tracked down several of the people behind it to New York and Brussels they told me that they were receiving between 125,000 and 200,000 unique hits every day; on a major news day that usually rose to a quarter of a million. The traffic in gory pictures is in both directions. Under the noses of the broadcast media, sites such as MySpace and YouTube are becoming the repository for gruesome images of war shot by American soldiers in Iraq and Afghanistan. Sometimes both sides even use the same pipes. For a long time the Islamic Army in Iraq used Yahoo's free online newsgroups to distribute their communiqués and videos to supporters; in May 2005 its files were found to have been posted on Yahoo using a California-based satellite internet service provider that was designed for exclusive use by the US military in Iraq. 'The enemies of Allah will continuously [try to close down] our website,' an official statement from the insurgents explained. 'We ask you to register for our mailing list so that you continue to receive the latest news of the Islamic Army in Iraq.'

Islamist groups also knew something about how to make their operations interactive, and about the cybernetic urge to have one's finger on the trigger. In November 2005 a Sunni insurgent group in central Iraq called the Army of the Victorious Sect announced an open online competition for the design of the organisation's new website. The lucky winner was to receive an unusual prize: 'The winner will fire three long-range rockets from any location in the world at an American military base in Iraq by pressing a button [on his computer] with his own blessed hand, using technology developed by the jihad fighters.' Within days of the announcement the response was so overwhelming that they were forced to extend the deadline for submissions.

In April 2002, three months before Paul Van Riper started playing Millennium Challenge, thousands of soldiers from the Israeli Defence Forces (IDF) massed on the outskirts of Nablus on the West Bank to try out an unusual military manoeuvre. What was distinctive about their approach, as we saw in Chapter 6, is that they forged their own unique series of paths through the city by blowing holes through the walls of its buildings. Dealing with a fragmented enemy made up of many different armed Palestinian factions, the response of the IDF was to test a wholly new mode of military engagement – one that relaxed operational command from headquarters in favour of allowing greater coordination, with the help of new communications technology, among the soldiers on the ground. The technique, as we saw, became known as 'walking through walls'. To the military strategists behind it, it was also an example of a brand new manoeuvre called swarming.

Military swarming had been the subject of conversations in military think-tanks for some time. Once again, its pioneers drew their inspiration from a high-tech interpretation of John Boyd's OODA loop. The idea of swarming was that, by letting individual soldiers talk to each other using mobile communication devices, information loops (or OODA loops) between troops would be tightened or shortened, encouraging greater fluidity of movement. As the soldiers in the swarm learned to coordinate their movements by passing electronic messages back and forth they would fuse into a indivisible, constantly shifting organism not unlike those observed in the natural world. The result of all this coordinated zigzagging, Boyd's followers believed, would enable them to thoroughly spook the enemy: to wriggle around and continually prod its defences and finally, having provoked it into laying bare its vulnerabilities – to swarm around it like an army of bees.

Like the idea that soldiers should learn to be more non-linear in their movements we looked at in Chapter 6, swarming was imported into the IDF by a military think-tank called the Operational Theory Research Institute (OTRI). The OTRI had been inaugurated in 1996 by an acclaimed Israeli military strategist and former Brigade General called Shimon Naveh, and was no ordinary military think-tank. It gathered doctoral researchers in political science, mathematics and philosophy from Tel Aviv University and was steeped less in military folklore than in terminology drawn from cybernetics, systems theory and the colourfully radical theories of French philosophers from the 1968 generation. The aim was to train Israeli soldiers for a new kind of urban battlefield in which they would be forced to make split-second decisions because the enemy could melt out of the civilian population and back again; a battlefield where they would need to spot the sudden appearance of a machine-gun from under the dress of a Palestinian fighter, or the strange gait of an old man walking towards a checkpoint armed with a suicide belt. It wasn't long before it drew the attention of military thinkers outside Israel and the OTRI began working closely with the American, British and Australian armed forces, and military conferences everywhere buzzed with discussions of its unconventional new manoeuvres.

American military officials, of course, had good reason to be interested in the activities of the OTRI. Not only were they still figuring out how to transform their armed forces with new technology, but US Army troops were bogged down in an insurgency of their own in Iraq. The top brass soon dropped their talk of using high-tech communications to lift the fog of war and began to brainstorm solutions to a problem they had failed to predict. With his experience of fighting against urban guerrillas, it made sense to consult Shimon Naveh. Like Paul Van Riper, Naveh was an admirer of John Boyd; to complete the circle, Van Riper included both Naveh and Boyd in a list of his most important military influences. Among the military analysts who met with Naveh on one of his trips to the United States were representatives from the RAND Corporation, one of the world's most influential military think-tanks. RAND had long been supportive of the idea of swarming, and had done much to bring it to a wider audience. Since the early nineties, two of its analysts, John Arquilla and David Ronfeldt, had been arguing that in the age of ubiquitous information hierarchical organisations like the US military would be no match for the flexible terror networks that it was up against, and that traditional war fighting was giving way to 'netwars' in which dispersed groups of individuals would use mobile phones and the internet to coordinate their attacks. If America was incapable of beating these new foes, the only thing for it was to join them and become a network itself. Their conviction was redoubled when they read that anti-globalisation protesters against the World Trade Organization's meeting in Seattle in 1999 had used mobile phones to outwit the centralised radio system of the police. New, networked phalanxes of activists and terrorists were massing in the shadows armed with little more than mobiles in their pockets, and knew how to swarm on their enemies and then disappear into thin air before they could be apprehended. If they were going to stand any chance of maintaining order and security, the authorities needed to keep up.

The problem was that coordination like this is fiendishly difficult to achieve. Imagine that my friend and I decide to go out for the evening. Before the advent of the modern communications era we would simply agree to meet at a particular location at a mutually convenient time. Now that we are both endowed with mobile phones, however, both of us can call each other with regular updates on our status and constantly revise those arrangements. Provided there are only the two of us there is no reason why this shouldn't go like clockwork. But what happens if it isn't just the two of us – what if everyone in our bowling club has made a loose arrangement to meet somewhere in town? Now we and all of our bowling companions have a choice. Either we can involve ourselves in e-mailing and texting everyone in the group to agree a series of meeting points and times, or we can simply leave it to a few people in the group to make the decisions and to co-ordinate everyone else. The reason why most people choose the latter is because peer-to-peer coordination requires constant communication among those who are involved in it, and makes any kind of manoeuvre complicated and time-consuming. Micro-ordination like this looks good on paper, and can be hugely enjoyable for the young people who spend their leisure time drifting around cities in huge shoals, making fleeting arrangements to meet one another. When a group needs to progress with any purpose towards a given objective, however, it tends to be worse than useless: people get so bogged down in messaging each other for updates that they are unable to make any headway.

The difficulties of coordinating human activity into an electronic swarm might help to explain why, when asked to stage a full-scale military operation during the Israeli–Hezbollah conflict of 2006, the eccentric manoeuvres of the OTRI seem to have backfired rather badly on the Israeli Defense Forces. In July 2006, after Hezbollah fighters seized two Israeli soldiers and stole them across the border into Lebanon, the IDF invaded Southern Lebanon. The invasion did not progress as they had expected. For a start, the Israeli Army seems to have become so convinced of its own military and technological superiority that it didn't think it would have to fight any 'real' wars any more. The IDF, as a result, relied too heavily on its air force to wipe out South Lebanon's infrastructure in the hope that Hezbollah's guerrillas would simply cave in. During the ensuing ground war, 'small but smart' mobile units of Israeli soldiers, which owed their origins to the twin ideas of network-centric warfare and military swarming, seemed unsure of what their aims were and where they were headed; the vast majority of their operations were embarrassing failures. In the official inquests into the war that followed the five-week invasion, military officials blamed the OTRI's complicated operational jargon and manoeuvres for many of its mistakes. During a meeting of the heads of Israeli military intelligence just prior to the incursion into Lebanon, for example, there were complaints that the army had stopped relying on Hebrew for its operational instructions, and that the dominant language was now 'gibberish'.

The OTRI was closed down and Shimon Naveh, who had already been removed from his job a month before the war began, was cast out of military favour. That might have been unfair, given that many of the decisions about how to conduct the war were made above his head. What we do know, however, is something about what he was up against. The Westerner currently most trusted by Hezbollah is a former British diplomat and spy called Alastair Crooke. Crooke, who worked as an agent of the British Secret Intelligence Service (MI6) before being seconded by Tony Blair to be the European Union's envoy to the Middle East between 1997 and 2003, now lives in Lebanon and spends his time encouraging discussions between Islamist movements and Western governments. After the 2006 war, he was taken to South Lebanon by Hezbollah officials and allowed rare access to its battlefield commanders. In October 2008 I visited him in Beirut and asked him what he had seen and heard. At the beginning of the 2006 war, Crooke told me, Hezbollah fighters were given general orders and were then broken down into tiny cells, each of which operated quite independently of any central command. A specialist team was given high-tech listening devices and managed, according to Crooke, to intercept electronic communications flying to and fro between IDF personnel. The bulk of Hezbollah's military units, however, were encouraged

to avoid unnecessary electronic chatter; when unit commanders did need to pass on messages they relied on relatively
primitive means such as motorcycle couriers.

Despite the fact that their OODA loop was not speeded up
by new communications technology and without the help of
complicated military manoeuvres, it is now generally accepted
that Hezbollah's fighters performed very well in the 2006 war,
and better than the IDF troops they were fighting against.
'Rather than have to react faster than the IDF's decision-cycle,'
one analysis of the war from Washington's Center for Strategic
and International Studies concluded, 'they could largely
ignore it, waiting out Israeli attacks, staying in positions, re-
infiltrating or re-emerging from cover, and choosing the time
to attack or ambush'. Just like Paul Van Riper, whose swarm of
patrol boats knocked a vastly superior force off balance during
that wargame in 2002, Hezbollah's commanders found that
giving their fighters clear and prior battle instructions was
vastly more important than allowing them to liaise with each
other electronically during the conflict itself. Faced with a
technologically superior enemy, both Van Riper and Hezbollah
seemed to understand, it was still possible to get inside your
enemy's information loop and confuse him. But only if those
under your command had a very clear idea of what was
expected of them; only if they ignored that enemy's information loop; and only if they switched off their mobile phones
and fell back on their own initiative.

Swarming wasn't the only way in which American military
strategists were borrowing from network theory to fight the
insurgency in Iraq. They were also using it to draw up maps of
those they were fighting against. In 2006 the Pentagon's

updated statement of its military doctrine and objectives included a section on 'irregular warfare' and how to use social network theory to trace the connections between insurgent groups. In December of the same year a newly revised and updated US Army and Marine Corps manual for fighting counterinsurgencies included an appendix on the same kind of social network analysis, complete with diagrams of nodes and the connections that tie them together. According to the army officer who helped pen the counter-insurgency manual, diagrams like this had helped the Army's 4th Infantry Division capture Saddam Hussein in December 2003. During the summer of that year intelligence analysts and commanders in the 4th Infantry Division had built 'link diagrams' of all of Saddam's relatives as well as military officers, drivers and other staff members. For the following months, analysts drew maps linking the various people involved in the former Iraqi leader's security detail, and of everyone related to him by blood or tribe. Amendments to the diagrams were made continually as more and more names of Saddam's cohorts were discovered. Raids were then planned to apprehend key individuals, which led to the capture of more of his associates higher up the chain of command, which in turn led to Saddam Hussein's hole in the ground.

Diagrams like this have long been used by police and security services looking to build up a picture of shadowy criminal organisations, and they can be very useful. The idea that we should become cartographers of the panoply of connections between things or people, as we saw earlier, has grown in its influence as we spend more of our time trying to navigate Cyburbia. This enthusiasm for pattern recognition is no bad thing; it can encourage us to make rapid associations and can quicken and thicken our appreciation of how densely inter-connected the world is. It can also be fun; on Facebook we can spend hours finding out which of our friends know each other and how they are all linked. There are, however, problems with joining up all the dots to see everything in terms of a computer network. In excavating maps of hidden connections we might be tempted to divine patterns where none exist. Before the sixties, as the French sociologists Luc Boltanski and Ève Chiapello point out, networks were usually considered to refer to clandestine, illegitimate, secret or illegal organisations that, although dispersed throughout the population, some-how maintained a private bond which gave them secret access to the levers of power. The outlandish conspiracy theories that now regularly find their way around the internet might have something to do with our predisposition to uncover patterns and associations behind apparently random events. Sometimes the alleged conspiracy even refers back to ties forged on the internet. When the Bridgend area of South Wales was cata-pulted to national attention by a spate of suicides of young people in 2007 and early 2008, Britain's media was quick to point to their use of social networking sites as the common fea-ture. Only after a judicial investigation officially discounted the idea that there was anything to link the deaths did rumours of an internet suicide pact begin to subside.

In much the same way, importing the analysis of networks into counter-insurgency and counter-terrorism could obscure as much as it disclosed. It wasn't long before some military ana-lysts were warning of the dangers. 'The counterinsurgent must resist imposing a meta-structure over the insurgency or attempting to identify a single leader,' advised one scholar in the US Army magazine *Military Review* in 2007. 'Identifying a single high-value target to kill . . . sets the counterinsurgent a difficult goal whose accomplishment requires prodigious resources that may produce only modest benefits.' When, shortly after Millennium Challenge, Paul Van Riper was asked how the new, network-based concepts that the wargame had been designed to champion could help with counter-terrorism, he had no hesitation in taking them down a peg. 'You cannot use the tools of systems analysis against soft systems, including some social systems,' he told one audience. 'I think it's social science run amok.'

Once again, Van Riper had a point. Just how an idea aimed at understanding computer networks could explain the complex affiliations in Iraq's largely tribal society was never properly explained by the military social network theorists. More importantly, and with such a motley collection of different insurgent groups making trouble for American troops there, the danger in subjecting them to a network analysis was that they would appear to be much more connected to each other, and with other Islamic militant groups around the world, than they really were. According to the network theorists who borrowed their terms from the analysis of computer and telephone systems, the power of any network lay not in the number of nodes in the system but in the number of connections between those nodes, which rose much more sharply than the number of nodes themselves to give rise to a network effect. As individual insurgents or insurgent groups sprung up in Iraq and beyond, the danger was that social network analysts would add up the nebulous ties between them to arrive at a single all-powerful enemy called the Al-Qaeda network.

*

If it doesn't make much sense to think of militant Islamic terrorism as having morphed into a global network, then what is it? A roundabout clue can be found by watching *The Thomas Crown Affair* – not the remake, but the original 1968 film with Steve McQueen and Faye Dunaway. Steve McQueen plays Thomas Crown, a world-weary millionaire art lover who gets a kick out of organising bank robberies. Crown's planning for his heists is a little unusual. He hires each of the robbers separately and anonymously, so that they are unable to identify either him or their accomplices, and has each of them loiter around different payphones just prior to the robbery to await their instructions. The bank robbers converge on the bank from different directions and then, as soon as the job is done, go their separate ways. That is the last they see of each other, or of Thomas Crown.

Nearly thirty years after it was made, an MIT-trained scientist from Washington called Jim Bell was thinking about *The Thomas Crown Affair* when he had an idea that he thought might overthrow every government in the world. Bell was an enthusiastic member of a loose online community of technologically aware anarchists who called themselves cypherpunks, and whose stated goal was to translate the freedoms that the internet had to offer into everyday life. For some time he had been mulling possibilities for using the internet to further the fight against big government, and before long he had hit on an idea that was as brilliant as it was chilling. In an essay that he posted to his fellow anarchists in 1995, Bell speculated as to whether it might be possible to set up an online lottery to solicit anonymous donations together with bets 'predicting' the death of certain US government officials, and then award all the winnings to the person who 'predicted' the day of their death correctly. If there were any doubt about the meaning of those inverted commas, Bell's essay was titled 'Assassination Politics'.

Jim Bell was very pleased with his idea, which struck him as an excellent way not only to deter people from working for the US government but of handing the administration of law and order back to the people. 'Imagine for a moment,' he wrote, 'that, as ordinary citizens were watching the evening news, they see an act by a government employee or officeholder that they feel violates their rights, abuses the public's trust or misuses the powers that they feel should be limited. What if they could go to their computers, type in the miscreant's name, and select a dollar amount: the amount they, themselves, would be willing to pay to anyone who "predicts" that officeholder's death. That donation would be sent, encrypted and anonymously, to a central registry organization and be totalled, with the total amount available within seconds to any interested individual. If 0.1 per cent of the population, or one person in a thousand, was willing to pay $1 to see some government slimeball dead, that would be, in effect, a $250,000 bounty on his head.' Like those peer-to-peer file sharing websites that sprang up after Napster was collared by the law, Bell suggested that the scheme might even be within the law. After all, donors of digital cash would only be offering gifts to those who predicted deaths correctly. As anonymous electronic peers, the identity of both donors and predictors would remain a secret both to each other and to the organisation itself, as would the date of their predictions. Moreover, since winners would be paid untraceable digital cash no one in the organisation would get to know their identity when they came along to claim their reward. The best thing about it, Bell tickled himself, was that no prosecutor would dare file charges against it for fear that his or her name might show up in the next lottery.

Bell was not quite right about the legality of a market for assassinations. In 1997 he was convicted of using false social security numbers; US government officials frankly admitted in conversations with court reporters that the real reason they wanted him put away was because they feared he might turn his idea for an assassination market into something more practical. Shortly after he was imprisoned, the cypherpunks mailing list was used to defend Bell and his assassinations market. Those threats were traced by federal prosecutors to a Canadian who, in 2001, was convicted of offering money online in return for anyone who could successfully 'predict' the deaths of several federal magistrates who had been involved in prosecuting Bell. In the same year yet another 'Assassination Politics' enthusiast surfaced in Australia. Using the pseudonym 'Professor Rat', he was found to have posted, among other things, a message on an Ohio website suggesting that a policeman who had recently killed an unarmed black suspect would make the perfect candidate for an assassination market.

The idea for an electronic assassination market was always too deranged and murderous to attract much of a following, but there was something about its modus operandi that sounded familiar. The way Bell talked about it in his essay, as a perfectly self-regulating system akin to a thermostat, harnessing the wisdom of crowds to find out which public officials most deserved to be killed by electronic diktat, made it sound like he had been reading Norbert Wiener. As Wiener understood it, remember, the essence of any cybernetic apparatus was that it would steer itself automatically via the continuous flow of messages and feedback around its system; like Bell, he had used a thermostat as one of his central examples. The striking thing about the 'Assassination Politics' cases was that there is no evidence that Jim Bell and the other enthusiasts ever knew each other well enough to conspire in developing an assassinations market. Based in different countries, each sprung independently from the electronic ether with an idea about how it could work and against who. Not only was there no conspiracy, but that was precisely the point: there could never be a conspiracy because the perfect anonymity of the system meant that none of those involved would ever get to know any of the others.

The 'Assassination Politics' cases made troubling reading for American law enforcement officials. The possibility of an assassination market, according to some accounts, is one reason why governments will never allow digital cash payments to be entirely untraceable, even though the technology for doing so is ready and waiting to be used. But what does it have to do with militant Islamic extremism? Only this: the anonymous coordination among strangers in Jim Bell's system is eerily analogous to the way in which violent Islamic extremism has evolved in the last few years. The closest thing radical Islamism has to a military strategist is a bearded, red-headed Syrian called Abu Mus'ab al-Suri. Before he was apprehended in Pakistan in 2005, al-Suri spent fifteen years putting together an insurgency manual for violent Islamic extremists called *The Call to Global Islamic Resistance*. He came to the conclusion that, facing an overwhelming enemy, the only way to continue the struggle was to jettison the idea of building a traditional, hierarchical terrorist organisation and instead rely on a shadow organisation made up of mobile, nomadic cells entirely unconnected to each other. Throughout his dense trea-

tise, al-Suri sounds like a marketing guru who has only
recently discovered what electronic 'buzz' can do to revitalise
the fortunes of an embattled product. He has spent years, he
informs his reader, seeking out a 'a method which the enemy
has no way of aborting, even when he understands the method
and its procedures, and arrests two-thirds of its operators. A
method which is susceptible to self-renewal and to self-per-
petuation as a phenomenon after all its conditions and causes
are present and visible to the enemy itself.' Just like Jim Bell,
what al-Suri discovered was that a new kind of terror movement could be propagated on the internet and perpetrated by
strangers who happen to roll up to heed the call – a self-steering system that, as soon as it was given a push, would take on
a life of its own.

Al-Suri's strategy for leaderless Islamic resistance was to
build a new kind of terror movement whose only claim to be a
network was that it was organised via the internet. To make
sure everyone got the message, in the years before he was
arrested al-Suri took the trouble to post his magnum opus all
over the web. Sure enough, since the invasions of Afghanistan
and Iraq most terror attacks by violent Islamic extremists have
had faint or zero connection with any central organisation
called Al-Qaeda. Instead, a new wave of jihadis has been
inspired largely by documents and manuals available online.
There has, concludes the counter-terrorism analyst Marc
Sageman, 'been a change from offline to online interaction in
the evolution of the threat . . . instead of traditional leaders
being in control of the global Islamist terrorist social movement, it is the unnamed followers who decide to act. The
leaders can then retrospectively award legitimacy to some of
these operations.' Even before he was arrested, al-Suri's new

strategy was producing results. From fewer than a hundred jihadi sites that existed prior to 11 September 2001 there are now nearly five thousand. The biggest single venue for the recruitment of Western youth into violent radical Islam, the expert on militant Islam Stephen Ulph told me, is not the mosque but the desktop computer. Just like those music file-sharing sites that are so good at dodging the authority of the music industry, the great advantage of the internet for radical Islamists is that it bypasses the authority of the local imam and puts angry young militants into direct communication with their peers.

When conventional armed forces like those of America or Israel tried to zap themselves into the information age by hitching their troops too tightly to electronic information, the result was often to make those troops jumpy and confused. Even worse, paying too much attention to the demands of that information loop could surrender the leadership and objectives of military organisations, leaving them rudderless but in constant touch with one another. In contrast, when there was little organisation at all to speak of, surrendering one's purpose to an electronic information loop and hoping for the best wasn't a bad kind of military strategy. The anonymous way in which traffic flows through Cyburbia can offer some cover for movements that need to give the authorities the slip, or that are so much in retreat that they are barely capable of organisation at all. The weak electronic ties that join together radical young Muslims sitting bored at their desktops, moreover, are enough to throw up a host of fruitful new connections and send extremist propaganda hurtling through Cyburbia. The result has all the makings of a new kind of online terror network, a kind of jihadi Facebook.

In some ways, of course, a military strategy like this is an admission of defeat. It lends the movement some resilience from attack, but only at the expense of denying it staying power and momentum. Neither is it entirely foolproof. Anti-terrorist officers from all the major security services, as we saw in Chapter 7, now spend much of their time with their ear to electronic chatter in order to map terror networks and predict when an attack might be in the offing. Even when one of this new wave of desktop jihadis does get through to plant a bomb, their lack of hands-on training often lets them down. The reason why so many of their bombs have failed to go off, Marc Sageman points out, is that most have been manufactured from unreliable material they have stumbled across on websites.

Afterword

Looping the Loop

The first person I ever poked on Facebook was the American actress Christina Ricci. I loved Ricci in the independent film *Buffalo 66*, enjoyed *The Opposite of Sex*, could even seen the merits of her performance in the crowd-pleaser *Sleepy Hollow* – and given that everyone was poking everyone else, it seemed churlish not to, though hooking up with a top Hollywood talent was always going to be a tricky. The day I poked Ricci and asked for her hand in friendship she was listed as having 3213 friends. If she wasn't full up already, it was going to take her a while to get around to someone like me.

There's something of the playground about Facebook, an instinctive, almost tribal urge to show off about how popular you are and who's in your gang. Since Facebook ties one's privacy settings to the acknowledgement of friendship, collecting friends there is an excellent way for the nosey to navigate the place. Then there is the difficulty involved in saying no to offers of electronic friendship; refusal often offends and the decision is mined with the potential for snubs and faux pas. Accept too many, however, and it defeats the purpose of having a private circle of friends. Add to this the fact that no one wants to be friendless and you have the recipe for a carnival of threadbare electronic friendship, especially among the young. A global study of eighteen thousand technology-savvy young people between fourteen and twenty-four published in 2007 discovered that they are, on average, connected to fifty-three people whom they consider to be online friends. Just six of those fifty-three were real-life close friends, the study found, while a further twenty-seven came from a wider circle of friendly acquaintances. The remaining twenty were purely online buddies: despite the fact that they had never met in person, the young people interviewed considered them proper friends.

These latter connections, forged between people on online social networks, are known to network theorists as our weak ties. Ray Pahl is professor of sociology at the University of Essex and an expert on the ties that bind us together. Pahl believes that a good deal of Facebook's phenomenal growth can be boiled down to simple demographics – the huge numbers of people who now leave the family home for some form of higher education. When the same young people leave university, he says, they want to recreate that cosy student environment, even when they're scattered around the world, and that's what Facebook does very well. As well as supporting our existing and real friendships, however, digital gadgetry can help to muddy their waters. Pahl told me the story of how he had been hired by a telecoms company to investigate how successful professionals use their BlackBerries and other e-mail machines. The plan was to interview them to find out how communication gizmos help keep them in touch with their extended network of friends and contacts wherever in the world they happened to find themselves. The sponsor was hoping for a breathless eulogy to the power of digital friendship, but Pahl's findings begged to differ. With little time on their hands, those who can afford it use technology to keep their acquaintances at bay, the better to concentrate on their real friends. Chortling at the annoyance of his sponsor, Pahl concluded that what most of us would really like is to separate the wheat from the chaff, to keep a small and valued group of friends close while using technology to discreetly manage the demands of the rest. It is when that distinction between real and imaginary friends collapses that problems arise, because it inevitably eats into the time we should be spending with our nearest and dearest. 'Anyone who thinks they've got two hundred friends', Pahl says, 'has got no friends.'

What use, then, are imaginary friends? One thing the explosion of weak electronic ties in places like Facebook has achieved is to make the most tantalising nostrum of social network theory – the idea that we are living in a small world – into a triumphant reality. When Stanley Milgram used the results of a letter-writing experiment to argue that each of us is only six degrees of separation away from anyone else on the planet back in 1967, he was only able to do so by taking liberties with the evidence. In August 2008, however, researchers from Microsoft made the historic announcement that in the age of electronic messaging the six degrees thesis had finally come to pass. The researchers had studied records of thirty billion electronic messages as they flew around the internet. They considered two people to have a connection if they had sent one another at least one electronic missive and concluded that each of us, on average, is linked by 6.6 degrees of separation.

It was, they told journalists, 'the first time a planetary-scale social network has been available'.

For all the bluster of the Microsoft researchers, it sounded as if the global electronic village had finally come around. It wasn't the first time that someone had thought to drag Milgram's small world experiment into the internet age. In 2003, in a study more faithful to the design of Milgram's own, the social network theorist Duncan Watts tested Milgram's hypothesis at Colombia University, using e-mail rather than letters and managed to reproduce his findings. The results made even more dispiriting reading for supporters of small world theory. Despite the relative ease of sending off an e-mail, less than 2 per cent of those e-mail letters forwarded onwards to friends and acquaintances ever arrived at their destination inbox, possibly because their recipients took them for spam or junk. It seemed that people didn't want to bother trying to navigate a network of weak electronic ties because they knew those ties were so weak as to be non-existent. We may well now be six electronic degrees of separation away from each other, but it is not going to do us much good any time soon. Online social networks such as Facebook make for an excellent way of mapping who knows whom and laying bare the connections between us. Just because we can take a bird's-eye view of our extended network on Facebook, it doesn't mean that that map of connections is going to take us anywhere or be useful for anything. Over forty years, network theorists had promised us that the presence of weak ties within any society would send information zipping around it and bring amazing new opportunities. When their hopes finally coalesced in an online social network that map of connections was only useful for gawping at. Even if we could make our way around a network of weak electronic ties it probably wouldn't get us very far. If the CIA were to try to use online networks to hook up with Osama bin Laden, Duncan Watts mused, they were probably going to come up short. 'The last couple of people in the chain,' he pointed out, 'are not going to be particularly cooperative, even if they could be.'

Of course, we Facebookers understand this already. After our initial introduction to the place and its orgy of transient friendship, most of us only want to bother with people at one degree of separation from ourselves. More than that, many of us secretly want to narrow down our range of electronic ties and make them more manageable. When too many others flood in we move on. Facebook does indeed give rise to a network effect, as its founder Mark Zuckerberg implied, and that network effect can be seen in the way that it uses its weak electronic ties to throw up a panorama of new connections. It's not us who benefit from this proliferation of weak ties but the network itself. With all these electronic ties at its disposal it can send information racing around itself with all the alacrity of a pinball machine. As everyone from marketers to terrorists now appreciates, our weak ties take on a life of their own in Cyburbia.

This place called Cyburbia, I've argued, has been nearly seventy years in the making, and online social networks are only its freshest and most dazzling embodiment. The architecture of Cyburbia can be traced to cybernetics, which reinterpreted life as a stream of messages on an information loop and saw the defining feature of everything as its ability to respond to a continuous cycle of instruction and feedback. Cybernetics started out as little more than a metaphor or an heuristic device, a way of understanding how man and machine could work together in a single information loop to operate a more responsive anti-aircraft missile system in the middle of the Second World War. Through a complicated series of manoeuvres the cybernetic metaphor inched closer to reality. It helped that its ethos was borrowed by a new generation of activists in the late sixties, many of whom were inspired to put theory into practice by building computers and trying to hook them up. By the nineties, as the information loop between our computer and mouse opened up to include everyone else via the internet, cybernetics had found a new lease of life in the enormous power of computer networking. Finally many of us spontaneously queued up to offer ourselves as human nodes on those networks.

Those of us who have grown up in the shadow of cybernetics owe it a great deal. Just as Norbert Wiener had hoped when he thought through the relationship between anti-aircraft gunner and enemy airplane pilot, spending more of our time on an electrical information loop with its instantaneous cycle of instruction and feedback has made us more immediately responsive to information that comes our way. Flanked by squadrons of our electronic peers, we feel more confident in ducking around authority and figuring things out for ourselves. Having our myriad electronic ties at the ready teaches us to pay heed to a range of different opinions and to switch rapidly between them. Navigating through electronic information allows us much greater freedom of movement and encourages us to forge our own path rather than the one laid out for us. As our enthusiasm for life on an electronic information loop has spread outwards into the culture it has influenced our very sense of perspective and given us some thrilling new ways of looking at the world.

Architecture, however, frames and limits our movement as we walk around a place as well as eases it, and one can't help but notice that this place called Cyburbia hasn't quite turned out as its pioneers imagined. The electronic village of authentic communication and perfect understanding long promised by the gurus of cybernetics is as far away as ever. Trusting in our electronic peers leaves us vulnerable to those whose opinions are wrong-headed or whose motives are less than benign. The electronic ties we use to send information often spread gossip and misinformation. Our cybernetic habit of rapidly responding to messages and forwarding them on to the information conveyor belt as soon as they arrive can get us into trouble. The peer-to-peer architecture started out as a hippie *cri de coeur* at the conformism of post-war American life, but the layout of Cyburbia encourages us to conform to the opinion of our electronic peers. An idea designed to help us burrow under the purview of the authorities ends up storing our innermost thoughts on banks of computer servers. Our relentless activism when confronted with information can leave us unable to sit back and let things wash over us. Being at the beck and call of an information loop means that we often find it difficult to call a halt to our electronic exchanges and leaves us open to constant interruption. The map that we were promised we could use to find our way around the electronic village doesn't take us very far, and often gets us lost. Given license to cultivate what Marshall McLuhan called 'our revulsion against imposed patterns', we often end up imagining patterns which are not really there. Moreover, when organisations in the real world try to mimic the structure of Cyburbia or cosy up to its inhabitants they often end up getting distracted and wandering around in a daze.

At least some of the secret of the way that Cyburbia has developed lies deep within cybernetics itself and the problems that it set itself to solve. In retrospect, it seems a little alarming to extract a general theory of human nature from the battle of wills between a combat pilot and an anti-aircraft gunner during the Second World War. In a game of strategy between a bomber pilot and an anti-aircraft gunner, both parties need to make split-second decisions, and to remain highly responsive to a continuous loop of information about both their own direction and line of fire, and that of the enemy. In our daily lives most of us do not need to jump around so readily in response to an information loop. When Norbert Wiener argued that the exchange of messages was central to understanding society, and that messages sent between humans and between machines were fundamentally the same, he did us all a disservice. The communication that we have when we chat face-to-face does indeed deliver messages, and in theory those messages could be shipped back and forth in little electronic packets, but it does so within a series of visual cues and a broader context that are essential to understanding what we mean. As anyone who has ever tried to have a proper conversation by text or e-mail knows, the exchange of messages on an information loop is usually less than satisfactory and sometimes never-ending. Just as friendships cannot be forged on online social networks alone, neither, as we saw in the discussion of how the military has tried to borrow from cybernetics, can the flow of information around an electronic loop ever replace real intelligence, strategy or leadership. Information can be transferred into digital bits and passed around at dizzying speeds. Knowledge isn't so portable. It takes a little longer to be worked up and can only be ferried around by someone who knows what they are talking about. Information can often be contradictory, but knowledge is usually more reliable than that.

Maybe the architects of Cyburbia simply expected too much. For different reasons, Norbert Wiener, Marshall McLuhan and Stewart Brand all ended up attributing a kind of unearthly power to electronic communication. Writing in the dark aftermath of the Second World War and the Holocaust, Wiener convinced himself that human society was in danger of spiralling out of control and that only by planting information feedback loops throughout it could we prevent ourselves from careering towards collapse. In the late sixties, a new generation of veterans from the counter-culture borrowed cybernetics to fill the vacuum left by their radical politics, hoping that if only everyone could be put back into direct communication it would raise awareness of our common humanity. For a devoutly religious intellectual like Marshall McLuhan, the coming global electronic village was anticipated with all the fervour of divine revelation. This wasn't, of course, the first time that a new technology for communication had seemed so powerful as to take on metaphysical implications. In 1844, when Samuel Morse sent his first long-distance telegraph from Washington to Baltimore, so awed was he by the experience that he wondered aloud: 'What has God wrought?' Almost as soon as the electrical telegraph appeared physiologists began to compare its transmitters to human nerve endings, its messages to human thoughts and the entire telegraph network to a new kind of central nervous system. Much the same kind of rapturous confusion between man and electrical machine explains the phantoms that have grown up around our new communications technology. Just because we are electronic peers in Cyburbia it doesn't mean that the world is really flat, and does nothing to alleviate inequalities in the real world. Just because activists can sometimes use the internet and mobile phones to duck under the radar of authority it does not make them a panacea: when pro-democracy protesters in Belarus began using mobile phones to mount inventive demonstrations in the public spaces of Minsk, for example, the Belarussian authorities simply flicked a switch and blocked mobile phone coverage in those areas.

The deeper flaw in cybernetics lies in its rarefied understanding of what it is to be human. In the forties Norbert Wiener believed that the new electrical machines such as computers had become so complex that a new kind of language was needed to explain the workings of both man and machine. For his new language of messaging and feedback, what was most important was an ability to cycle through an information feedback loop, to constantly regulate one's own operation by adapting oneself to one's environment and one's effect on that environment. When an electrical system is designed to automatically regulate its operation through an information feedback loop, what it achieves is a state called homeostasis. Any homeostatic system makes it its priority to keep itself running smoothly and maintain some kind of equilibrium. Wiener himself gave the example of a thermostat – a thermostat within a sophisticated heating system relies on a continuous stream of feedback about the heat it is giving out so as to maintain a stable temperature.

When Wiener first unveiled his theory of cybernetics he was worried that our social system was on the brink of chaos and in need of giant information loops to act as its stabilisers. Now that his electrical information loop is finally up and running it turns out that the really fragile and unpredictable thing is the way that information passes through that loop, which is why it needs to be knitted together with all that feedback. Compared to that, in fact, we humans are surprisingly resilient. Wiener was right about the need to learn from our mistakes through continual feedback. He was, however, wrong to imagine that his feedback loop is the most vital weapon in our armoury. Planting myriad feedback loops within an electrical system keeps it ticking over very nicely, but the effort it expends on keeping itself stable leaves no time for anything more ambitious. What distinguishes us as humans is not that we are capable of cycling through an endless feedback loop but that we can progress with some kind of purpose. Pay too much attention to that information loop and the danger is that we lose sight of the reason why we are there in the first place. Like a wind-up toy placed on the floor, we go around in circles.

The irony is that Norbert Wiener the polymath was clever enough to know this all too well. He worried that if we relied too heavily on technology we might end up surrendering our sense of purpose and becoming appendages to an electrical machine. One of the reasons why Wiener was so enthusiastic about cybernetics is because it promised to automate all kinds of menial tasks and free us up for higher things. Just like those professionals interviewed by Ray Pahl, he hoped that technology would take care of our more mundane chores so that we could have more time for the stuff which really mattered. As if to reinforce his hope that the theory would be used to enhance rather than smother human purposes, Wiener borrowed the idea of cybernetics from the Greek word *kybernetes*, meaning 'helmsman' or 'pilot'. At least partly thanks to Wiener's work, combat pilots now have access to sophisticated on-board systems that quietly relieve them of lower-level functions so they can concentrate on more pressing matters. We inhabitants of Cyburbia have no such luck. Connected to our electrical information loop for long periods, ferrying information back and forth between ourselves, we have no automated system at our disposal. The system is certainly self-steering and running on autopilot, but only because it has us as its automatons, darting around through information clouds in response to an endless stream of instruction and feedback.

As nodes on networks patched together out of weak ties, hitched slavishly to an electronic information loop, we humans are not as powerful as we think. But that is not the only way to think about our attachment to electronic information. Just as books and television have changed us, the time that we spend adjusting ourselves to electronic information and feeding back information of our own has delicately changed our sensibilities over the last thirty years. Introduced into our culture via video games, mobile phones and the internet, it has helped to make us more responsive to information, more agile and associative in our thinking, more curious to find things out on our own, more capable of switching in and out of different streams of information and more stubbornly determined to forge our own path through information. Many of us, as a result, are tired of the old ways of doing things and are looking for something more intense, more oblique and more involving. Rather than surrender ourselves to this new sensibility, those of us with something to say can do things with it. If we are to capture the attention of those who have grown up living their lives on an electronic information loop, we will have to.

Cybernetics has brought us a long way, but now that its global information loop is fully built it is in danger of leaving us lost. Its gurus were so mesmerised by the medium that they made the mistake of trying to push us into it head first, of trying to remake us in its image rather than the other way around. Now we need to spend some time thinking about the message. The book took off not because its early evangelists went around waving them in people's faces or attesting to their incredible power but because talented authors took the trouble to master this new way of working and to write great books. In the same way, our brilliant new technology for communication is still young and we are only just getting the hang of it. Just like teenagers growing up in post-war suburbia many of us inhabitants of Cyburbia are growing bored, and are longing to be transported somewhere more exciting. If we use the medium for our own purposes rather than following slavishly in its thrall, we can imagine new ways of working, exciting new kinds of art and culture, new ways of organising ourselves and getting things done. What we need now are new storytellers capable of awakening our interest with narratives that allow us greater freedom of movement, employers canny enough to give us tasks that absorb our divided attention, teachers clever enough to whet our appetite for making associations, guides bold enough to take us by the hand through the fog of electronic information and show us something new.

Switch off that information loop for a while, because you don't need it as much as you think. Take a deep breath and then blast that buzzing, zigzagging infernal enemy aeroplane right out of the sky.

Select Sources and Recommendations for Further Reading

Chapter 1: The Loop

Conway, Flo and Jim Siegelman, *Dark Hero of the Information Age: In Search of Norbert Wiener, The Father of Cybernetics* (New York: Basic Books, 2005)

Heims, Steve Joshua, *Constructing a Social Science for Postwar America: The Cybernetics Group, 1946–1953* (Cambridge, MA: MIT Press, 1991)

————, *John von Neumann and Norbert Wiener: From Mathematics to the Technologies of Life and Death* (Cambridge, MA: MIT Press, 1980)

Wiener, Norbert, *The Human Use of Human Beings: Cybernetics and Society* (New York: Avon Books, 1950)

Chapter 2: The Peer

Caute, David, *'68: The Year of the Barricades* (London: Hamish Hamilton, 1988)

Kurlansky, Mark, *1968: The Year That Rocked the World* (London: Jonathan Cape, 2004)

Menn, Joseph, *All the Rave: The Rise and Fall of Shawn Fanning's Napster* (New York: Crown Business, 2003)

Turner, Fred, *From Counterculture to Cyberculture: Stewart Brand, the Whole Earth Network and the Rise of Digital Utopianism* (Chicago: University of Chicago Press, 2006)

Chapter 3: The Tie

Barbrook, Richard, *Imaginary Futures: From Thinking Machines to the Global Village* (London: Pluto Press, 2007)

Gordon, W. Terrence, *Marshall McLuhan: Escape into Understanding* (Toronto: Stoddart Publishing, 1997)

Joselit, David, *Feedback: Television Against Democracy* (London: MIT Press, 2007)

Marchand, Philip, *Marshall McLuhan: The Medium and the Messenger* (Cambridge, MA: MIT Press, 1989)

McLuhan, Marshall, *The Gutenberg Galaxy: The Making of Typographic Man* (London: Routledge & Kegan Paul, 1962)

————, *Understanding Media: The Extensions of Man* (London: Routledge & Kegan Paul, 1964)

Turkle, Sherry, 'Always-on/Always-on-you: The Tethered Self', in James Katz (ed.), *Handbook of Mobile Communication Studies* (Cambridge, MA: MIT Press, 2008)

Chapter 4: The Network Effect

Bayard, Pierre (trans. Jeffrey Mehlman), *How to Talk About Books You Haven't Read* (London: Granta, 2008)

Boltanski, Luc and Ève Chiapello (trans. Gregory Elliott), *The New Spirit of Capitalism* (London: Verso, 2005)

Flichy, Patrice (trans. Liz Carey-Libbrecht), *The Internet Imaginaire* (Cambridge, MA: MIT Press, 2007)

Maier, Corinne, *Bonjour Paresse: De l'art et la nécessité d'en faire le moins possible en enterprise* (Paris: Editions Michalon, 2004)

Mitchell, William J., *Me++: The Cyborg Self and the Networked City* (London: MIT Press, 2003)

Shirky, Clay, *Here Comes Everybody: The Power of Organising Without Organisations* (London: Allen Lane, 2008)

Watts, Duncan J., *Six Degrees: The Science of a Connected Age* (London: Heinemann, 2003)

Chapter 5: Peer Pressure

Benkler, Yochai, *The Wealth of Networks: How Social Production Transforms Markets and Freedom* (London: Yale University Press, 2006)

De Zengotita, Thomas, *Mediated: How the Media Shape the World Around You* (London: Bloomsbury, 2007)

Howe, Jeff, *Crowdsourcing: How the Power of the Crowd is Driving the Future of Business* (London: Random House Business Books, 2008)

Jennings, David, *Net, Blogs and Rock 'n' Roll: How Digital Discovery Works and What it Means for Consumers, Creators and Culture* (London: Nicholas Brealey, 2007)

Keen, Andrew, *The Cult of the Amateur: How Today's Internet is Killing our Culture and Assaulting our Economy* (London: Nicholas Brealey, 2007)

Solove, Daniel J., *The Future of Reputation: Gossip, Rumor and Privacy on the Internet* (New Haven: Yale University Press, 2007)

Sunstein, Cass R., *Republic.com 2.0* (Princeton: Princeton University Press, 2007)

Chapter 6: Non-Linear

Calvino, Italo, *Six Memos for the New Millennium* (London: Jonathan Cape, 1992)

Castronova, Edward, *Synthetic Worlds: The Business and Culture of Online Games* (Chicago: University of Chicago Press, 2005)

Johnson, Steven, *Everything Bad is Good For You: How Popular Culture is Making us Smarter* (London: Allen Lane, 2007)

Salen, Katie and Eric Zimmerman, *The Rules of Play: Game Design Fundamentals* (Cambridge, MA: MIT Press, 2004)

Weinberger, David, *Everything is Miscellaneous: The Power of the New Digital Disorder* (New York: Times Books, 2007)

Weizman, Eyal, *Hollow Land: Israel's Architecture of Occupation* (London: Verso, 2007)

Chapter 7: Multiplicity

Battelle, John, *The Search: How Google and its Rivals Rewrote the Rules of Business and Transformed our Culture* (London: Nicholas Brealey, 2005)

Carr, Nicholas, 'Is Google Making Us Stupid?', *The Atlantic*, July/August 2008

Halavais, Alexander, *Search Engine Society* (Cambridge: Polity, 2008)

Wiener, Norbert, *Cybernetics, Or Control and Communication in the Animal and the Machine* (Cambridge, MA: MIT Press, 1948)

Chapter 8: Feedback

Siegel, Lee, *Against the Machine: Being Human in the Age of the Electronic Mob* (New York: Spiegel & Grau, 2008)

Van Doren, Charles, 'All the Answers: The Quiz Show Scandals – and the Aftermath', *The New Yorker*, 28 July 2008

Chapter 9: Network Failure

Arquilla, John and David Ronfeldt (eds), *Networks and Netwars: The Future of Terror, Crime and Militancy* (Santa Monica: RAND, 2001)

Berkowitz, Bruce D., *The New Face of War: How War Will be Fought in the 21ˢᵗ Century* (New York: Free Press, 2003)

Coram, Robert, *Boyd: The Fighter Pilot Who Changed the Art of War* (Boston: Little, Brown, 2002)

Cordesman, Anthony H., *Preliminary 'Lessons' of the Israeli–Hezbollah War* (Washington, DC: Center for Strategic and International Studies, 2006)

Hirsch, Gal, 'On Dinosaurs and Hornets – A Critical View on Operational Moulds in Asymmetric Conflicts', *RUSI Journal*, vol. 148, no. 4, August 2003

Kober, Avi, 'The Israel Defense Forces in the Second Lebanon War: Why the Poor Performance?', *Journal of Strategic Studies*, 31:1, 2008, pp. 3–40

Lia, Brynjar, *Architect of Global Jihad: The Life of Al-Qaida Strategist Abu Mus'ab al-Suri* (London: Hurst, 2008)

Osinga, Frans P. B., *Science, Strategy and War: The Strategic Theory of John Boyd* (London: Routledge, 2007)

Sageman, Marc, *Leaderless Jihad: Terror Networks in the Twenty-First Century* (Philadelphia: University of Pennsylvania Press, 2008)

Woodward, Bob, *Plan of Attack* (London: Simon & Schuster, 2004)

Afterword: Looping the Loop

Bowker, Geof, 'How to be Universal: Some Cybernetic Strategies, 1943–70', *Social Studies of Science*, vol. 23, no. 1, 1993, pp. 107–27

Brown, John Seeley and Paul Duguid, *The Social Life of Information* (Boston: Harvard Business School Press, 2000)

Goldsmith, Jack and Tim Wu, *Who Controls the Internet?: Illusions of a Borderless World* (New York: Oxford University Press, 2006)

Standage, Tom, *The Victorian Internet: The Remarkable Story of the Telegraph and the Nineteenth Century's Online Pioneers* (London: Weidenfeld & Nicolson, 1998)

Acknowledgements

Everyone has an opinion on what the new communication technologies are doing to us, and a good few of them were kind enough to give me benefit of their advice and their experience. Special thanks, however, to those who allowed themselves to be interviewed: Tim Berners-Lee, Tony Bilsborough, Adam Cox, Alastair Crooke, Ofra Graicer, Susan Greenfield, Hjalmar, Gloria Mark, Ray Pahl, Jonathan Sharples, Clay Shirky, Linda Stone, Stephen Ulph and Martin Westwell. Christophe Cauvy and Andrew Orlowski were very encouraging and made some excellent suggestions. Chapter 2 and the sections on Stewart Brand are hugely indebted to Fred Turner's original research in his book *From Counterculture to Cyberculture*. The case study of the Israeli incursion into Nablus in 2002 at the beginning of Chapter 6 is borrowed from Eyal Weizman's *Hollow Land*. The portrait of Norbert Weiner in Chapter 1 draws on Flo Conway and Jim Siegelman's biography of Weiner, *Dark Hero of the Information Age*. Likewise, the portrait of Marshall McLuhan borrows from W. Terrence Gordon's biography, *Escape into Understanding*, and the paragraphs about the career of Shawn Fanning are sourced from *All the Rave* by Joseph Menn.

The book owes its biggest debt to Adam Curtis; endlessly stimulating conversations with him over the years have helped to breathe life into the ideas here, and have taught me a great deal not only about cybernetics but about the art of story-telling. My agent Elizabeth Sheinkman nursed this idea from the beginning and without her galvanising enthusiasm I would never have got around to writing it down. The germs of many of the ideas here come from essays, articles and interviews I've written for the *Guardian* and the *Financial Times*, for which thanks go to editors Pilita Clark, Graham Watts, Peter Barber, Rosie Blau and Natalie Whittle on the *Financial Times*, and Toby Manhire and Janine Gibson at the *Guardian*. The staff at the ICA in London worked uncomplainingly around the leave of absence I took to write the book. Editors Tim Whiting, Stephen Guise, Zoë Gullen, Michael Schellenberg and Michelle MacAleese all worked on the manuscript at various stages of its production and their patient moulding of the material here helped to make the book much better than it would otherwise have been. Anna Goodman, Emma Harkin, James Harkin Senior, Aveen Treacy and Steven Foley deserve credit for their encouragement and sufferance while I was hunkered down writing. Unlike some of what goes on the internet, however, books are not an entirely collaborative enterprise; any errors are entirely my own.

Index